PRAISE FOR JOAN KENDALL'S *SECRETS ON SAULTER ROAD*

"I have been privileged to know Joan for many years as a friend and, most recently, as a patient. Reading her book was like being invited to sit on her back porch with a glass of tea and meeting the characters of her intriguing family.

"Her story is told with a courageous vulnerability that peels back social façades and carefully crafted niceties and lets the souls of the people spring to life. Walking down the interwoven paths of these family members reminds us that, while life is hard, the difficulties do not have to define us. We can choose redemption, even in the decisions that at the time may appear to be small, everyday things of life.

"Pull up your own chair with a glass of tea as you come close to the story of Joan's family, which is, in many ways, a picture of all our journeys."

WAYNE (BILL) KRUG, PHD
Practicing Clinical Psychologist
Birmingham, Alabama

D1157420

"Joan has written more than a mere memoir. It is a wonderful account of one who has experienced some of life's biggest challenges and who found the answers that all of us need. I hope her powerful story finds broad readership, not just among her friends, but also among the millions who are searching for life's real meaning and purpose."

SANDY WILLSON
Covenant Presbyterian Church
Birmingham, Alabama

"Joan takes us along her journey on Saulter Road from despair and heartache to a place of joy. The reader is left with great hope that no matter the course, one can rise above their circumstances. Her life is a great illustration that what happens to you is not as important as your reaction to what happens to you. The lessons learned within these pages apply to people of every age."

MARY GLYNN PEEPLES
Author, Speaker
Peeple's Passion, Worldwide podcast
Birmingham, Alabama

SECRETS
ON
SAULTER ROAD

SECRETS
ON
SAULTER ROAD

DISCOVERING HOPE AND FORGIVENESS IN THE WAKE OF MY TOXIC UPBRINGING

A MEMOIR

JOAN KENDALL

rush avenue press

Photos contained inside this book and the front cover image are from the private collection of the author.

Bible verses used in this book are quoted from the following versions: 21st Century King James Version, Holy Bible ©1994 Deuel Enterprises, Inc., and English Standard Version, The Holy Bible, Text Edition: 2016. ©2001 by Crossway Bibles, a publishing ministry of Good News Publishers.

Published by Rush Avenue Press, LLC
Contact: publisher@SecretsOnSaulterRoad.com
www.SecretsOnSaulterRoad.com

Paperback: 978-1-7338986-1-4
Hardcover: 978-1-7338986-2-1
Kindle: 978-1-7338986-3-8
EPUB: 978-1-7338986-4-5

Library of Congress Control Number: 2019903605
Cataloging in Publication Data on file with publisher.

Production and Marketing: Concierge Marketing Inc.
Printed in the United States of America.

10 9 8 7 6 5 4 3 2 1

To my eight grandchildren

with love and hope that they will walk in
wisdom as they navigate life.

CONTENTS

INTRODUCTION

I KNOW WHY YOUNG CHILDREN WATCH THE SAME MOVIE again and again or desire a favorite bedtime story night after night. Children need the familiar, the security that allows them to predict what comes next. As a child, I longed for the familiar; I, too, sought the comfort predictability yields.

But why now? Why, in my twilight years, have I watched the films *Life Is Beautiful* and *Babe* multiple times? *Life Is Beautiful* portrays a father who goes to great lengths to protect his son from the horrors of the Holocaust, and *Babe* is the story of a little pig's rescue from certain death.

Why have I repeatedly buried myself in Edna St. Vincent Millay's poem "Renascence" and Kermit's song, *The Rainbow Connection*?

The song of a frog resonates with me. Frogs croak, but Kermit croons. He serenades of a "sweet sound" calling his name, a voice heard "too many times to ignore it," and he foresees resolution in the end. "Someday we'll find it, the rainbow connection...."

Someday, indeed.

In one sense, my story is Everyman's: life is hard and then you die. However, in between, I learned that one lamentable decision can afflict and harm a family for many years. The repercussions of a single regrettable choice my mother felt compelled to make left no aspect of our lives untouched. Although each family member struggled differently, the pattern of our lives grew predictable, but not the kind of predictability that engenders stability and consolation.

I've thought about how I coped with trauma resulting from my mother's alcoholism, over which I had no control. I've pondered why I then inflicted hardship and brokenness upon myself and others. I do not have all the answers; in fact, I have many questions.

I write of what I know, though few realize how conflicted I became with risks versus benefits of telling my story. My two sisters and I were soldiers in the same domestic war, and few fighters want to reveal their combat experiences. Ultimately, the three of us decided that any benefit to the reader outweighed other concerns—although, by dredging up my memories, I risked stepping precariously close to the precipice of self-absorption and never returning.

However, the reverse occurred as I sorted through my family members' temperaments, complexities, circumstances, and choices. Walking in each character's shoes day after day, I came away with a greater appreciation that no person is one-dimensional; no one should be defined by a flaw or strength, or by an action or choice.

Perhaps I'll never understand the utility of the statement: "Children are resilient," except to comfort another's broken heart or excuse one's own hurtful behavior. I was not resilient—not until resolution stared me in the face.

1

MARY POPPINS OR CRUELLA DE VIL?

CROUCHED ON THE RUG IN FRONT OF OUR BLACK-AND-white television, eyes fixed on the screen, I watched some stranger mimic my mother. He staggered about the saloon, slurred his words, and picked a fight. A second cowboy swaggered in, and his opening words, "Looks like ole Jeb's had too much to drink," echoed through my five-year-old mind.

Then, I got it! *Something Mama drinks causes her to stumble, messes up her speech, and makes our family sad.* This was my first attempt at solving the puzzle. I didn't understand why Mother slept on the den sofa or talked on the kitchen phone most of the time, but I knew whatever she drank had something to do with it. Whatever it was made Daddy angry, and Mother responded in kind. And whatever she drank took her away from me.

Jadie Bell Thomas, our upstairs maid, stood in the gap each weekday. She nurtured and loved me for over thirteen years. Acting in loco parentis, Jadie Bell protected me and my two sisters, Linda and Susan, and although she loved us as her own, she couldn't rid our home of gloom and shame.

Heaven knows she tried. And if she'd known how to drive a car, she would have shouldered even more maternal duties—tasks Mama couldn't or wouldn't perform. Still, Jadie Bell was a pillow on which I could land and a faithful comrade in battle.

As preschoolers, my best friend Diane McCleskey and I spent most days roaming the woods, looking for crawdads in the streams, making bracelets out of dandelion stems, and playing outside until dinner. Excited to show Mother a four-leaf clover one day, we ran to the house only to be halted at the kitchen screen door. Jadie Bell intervened and gave the all-too-familiar look and tilt of the head, warning me to cease and desist. I knew the gesture's meaning well: Mother was acting like that man on TV.

Jadie Bell had our backs like any good soldier when Mama was drunk. So I quickly altered our course to distract Diane. "Last one to the swing is a rotten egg!" Diane and I were safely swinging, playing kickball, and squishing our toes in the sandbox that was nestled in the middle of three waist-high rock walls. We were safe because no one went into the house, and Jadie Bell kept Mother from charging out.

But I dreaded going inside for dinner that night.

"Hold your shoulders up, Elinor!" Daddy admonished Mama, his face flushed and his voice forceful. "Relax your brow, Elinor!" The tension devoured any hunger I brought to the kitchen table, but Jadie Bell was there, at least until after dinner. Daddy respected Jadie Bell and wanted her respect in return, so he kept the full force of his disappointment and anger in check while in her presence.

In the mornings or on rare afternoons when sober-mom appeared, the atmosphere lightened and Jadie Bell felt free to let down her guard. On one of those afternoons, during one of my younger sister's terrible-two temper tantrums, Mama threatened a visit from the boogeyman.

Susan's behavior worsened. "Elner," as Jadie Bell called Mama, "you better make good on your threat! Go put on Mr. Sax's coat and hat and come scare her. It'll serve her right."

"Oooooooh, clever idea, but I'll take it up a notch."

The scheme sounded exciting to me at age seven, until I watched fun-loving Mama take the prank to the next level. In addition to Daddy's trench coat and hat, she donned work boots and pulled a silk stocking over her face. The stocking flattened her nose and disguised her eyes as scary little slits. As Jadie Bell, Susan, and I played in the basement, sure enough, in came the boogeyman. While Susan cried and repented, our cur dog Sadie scurried so fast she slid across the floor on all fours and hit the wall.

I now think "Elner" overacted a bit, but it didn't harm Susan. The boogeyman's bursting onto the scene improved her behavior once and for all—or maybe she outgrew the terrible twos as children do.

Mama was a lady from the ground up and second to none when it came to charm and beauty. Throughout her life, with no effort at all, she maintained an ideal weight and an enviable hour-glass figure. She was classic looking and stood five foot five with a complexion that grew paler as the years passed.

Mama struck quite a pose. She remained a natural brunette throughout life and kept her high school hairstyle, just a bit shorter. A small bundle near her forehead created a puffy wave higher than the rest, close to her head, with curls on the ends like the famous actresses of the 1940s. Passing styles and peer pressure didn't sway Mama.

After completing Phillips High School in Birmingham, Alabama, Mother worked as a commercial artist before her employment with J.F. Knox Photography as Mr. Knox's assistant. His clients were primarily the successful businessmen and distinguished women of Birmingham. Mama's exposure to the crème de la crème of society may have helped cultivate her sense of style.

Mother enjoyed telling the story of a particularly distinguished lady who incessantly complained about the way her eyes appeared in the photographs. Put off, Mr. Knox finally blurted, "Well, ya knew you were cockeyed when ya came in here, didn't ya?" The woman was indignant, but Mama admired his quick, clever comeback—an adeptness they both shared.

Our unassuming mother never told us Mr. Knox entered her in the 1939 Queen of Vulcan contest, a onetime event celebrating the placement of the iron statute atop Red Mountain, overlooking the city. "Nearly every store in Downtown Birmingham promoted its own princess to compete in the pageant," reported *The Birmingham News* on September 6, 2007. Though not crowned queen, Mother was elected one of twenty-four ladies of the court.

My sisters and I learned of Mother's honor from my middle daughter. While thumbing through a local magazine's retrospective story in 2007, Meg's attention focused on a full-page 1939 photograph of the ladies of the court, and her lifetime affinity for old pictures prompted further scrutiny. "That's my grandmother!" Below the photograph were the young ladies' names, confirming Meg's quick recognition of a grandmother who never lost her beauty.

Linda and Susan and I were stunned to learn that throughout her sixty-six years, Mama never once mentioned the Queen of Vulcan contest. When Meg brought me the magazine, I studied the picture. *Mama doesn't look as happy and enthusiastic as the other girls, and I think I know why.*

Though Mother only dropped hints here and there, I pieced the puzzle together. Mother said more than once, "My best friend Jeanne Cooper was accidentally killed in a regatta race when we lived in Maryland."

Life had held promise in Chestertown, Maryland, in 1938, and college lay in her future. But before Mother turned seventeen, her mother divorced her "mean husband" and moved with her daughter and son to Birmingham to live with family, so their funds were scarce. Instead of bounding off to college, Mama was bound to work. She would have preferred a college life with her wealthy friends back in Maryland rather than work for Mr. Knox or be promoted as his "princess."

My nineteen-year-old mother met her thirty-year-old future husband at the Seven Seas restaurant in Birmingham. He and his partner, Doug Palmer, were hammering out plans during dinner for their new business venture when in walked my grandmother, Lydia Russell, and her daughter, Elinor. Doug recognized his friends Lydia and Elinor, introduced them to his friend, Sax Lawrence, and ended with Sax's desire to get to know Elinor better.

The next day, he phoned the Russell home. "This is Sax Lawrence. May I speak with Ms. Russell?"

"Just a moment," their maid responded, unsure of which Ms. Russell to summon. Her expression and gestures communicated, *I don't know what to do!*

"What's the matter, Ludie?" several family members asked at once.

"Mr. Lawrence is asking for Ms. Russell, but I don't know which one he wants." Sax, considerably older than Elinor and considerably younger than Lydia, waited patiently throughout the confusion and hushed discussion.

"You should have asked which one. Now what do we do?"

Weighing all options, Ludie handed the phone to "Miss" Russell. Bingo!

Elinor Russell, born in 1921, to Lydia and William Frazier Russell of Chestertown, Maryland, wed Gershon Saxton Lawrence on December 26, 1941, at the Episcopal Church of the Advent in Birmingham.

After ten months of marriage, Mother gave birth to my sister Linda. I followed five years later with Susan five years behind me—five years' difference when one is young is almost akin to being an only child.

*My parents on their
wedding day, 1941.*

*Mother as a
young lady.*

Me, age six.

Susan, age two.

Linda, age eleven.

When it came to literature, philosophy, or poetry, Mama was soulful and showed a serious side, with respect to the King's English. For an audience of one or two, she read Carl Sandburg's poems or recited "Little Boy Blue," a sad poem by Eugene Field about the death of a child and the faithfulness of his toys. Together, she and I listened to Lynn Fontanne's 1940 recording of "The White Cliffs." "I knew John was dead," Mama repeated with the slow alto voice of Ms. Fontanne.

"I need the number of Carl Sandburg, please," Linda and I heard our tight-as-a-tick mother tell the operator one night. *There's no way on earth she's gonna get through to this famous Pulitzer Prize–winning poet. No way!* "He lives in Flat Rock, North Carolina," Mama informed the operator. Linda and I raced to the extension. This would be worth our eavesdropping.

"Hello."

"Hello, Mr. Sandburg, my name is Elinor Lawrence, calling from Alabama. I'd like to talk with you about one of your poems."

"Felner, I don't take calls from strangers to discuss my poetry."

"No, it's Elinor." Changing course, she began reading the poem.

"Stop right there!" he demanded as Mama audaciously launched into her interpretation of his poem. "Felner, I know what it means. I wrote it. I'm going to hang up now."

Click.

"It's Elinor…" Mama faded out like fog.

Sixteen-year-old Linda thought the incident priceless, but I didn't. At the age of eleven, I felt shame and embarrassment for her, although it didn't seem to bother Mother, for she was back on the phone at the kitchen booth a minute later with who knows who.

Despite that bizarre but poignant scene, Mama passed down to me a love of poetry. The same love of poetry came from my maternal grandmother—we affectionately called her Buddie—a blue-ribbon winner for her poem, "Antiquity of Dust." Grabbing a cup of coffee and her cigarettes, Buddie jetted toward her typewriter daily to compose anecdotes and poetry before notions of housework or getting dressed interrupted her momentum.

Buddie, a dreaming elf, flourished in the world of words, her fingers flying through the keys with metaphors, similes, rhymes, and myriad other creative thoughts. Nothing rivaled her writing, and I became the beneficiary of all she produced—some typed, some handwritten scraps of paper found in boxes—even a published book of scores of her poems our Great Aunt Amy (Buddie's sister) published after Buddie's death. Mother bequeathed all of Buddie's poems and witty anecdotes to me. I loved them then and cherish them now.

Buddie lived with us for a brief period when I was fourteen and witnessed our home life firsthand—Daddy's nagging and absence, Mother's drinking, and the bickering between them. She later wrote of her observations and the effects on my sisters and me, but the letter wasn't discovered until 2018.

Buried in a box in her attic, Susan found the undated, twenty-three-page handwritten letter Buddie wrote us girls many years ago, most likely soon after her stay with us in 1961, since Buddie noted Linda was married. We had never seen the letter—this ghostlike dispatch from the past—so I sped to Susan's where we studied my grandmother's reflections:

[Excerpted from letter]
I don't know what lies before my own little daughter, but you girls rally around and give her well-deserved happiness.... I'd like my young daughter to be appreciated. Strive as she might to accomplish more than could be and always doing a good job, her reward has been criticism—and

finally, I fear, frustration. Surely her husband has many fine virtues, but the worst of his sins is eternal nagging. "Why didn't you do this? Why didn't you do that?"

The childish fits of rage he goes into for small reasons. The language before the children. The dreadful names he calls my daughter. Older by eleven years than she, he expected her from the first to be expert in every way. And, oh, how she broke my heart trying. A fiddle string can only be stretched so far before it breaks—I can't talk to the man.

He says my daughter "drinks"; is an alcoholic, etc. Yes, she drinks. It started after *the marriage.*

Joan wants to go to Southern California to college. Enough to show that she welcomes distance from a constantly bickering, criticizing atmosphere. She loves her family and the love hurts her.

Linda eloped young, and I know for the same reason. Linda is a fighter. She has much of her father's fire in temper, but I believe she has married well... But, by golly, he won't be allowed to dominate her.

Susan, the angel on earth, already has a look of puzzlement and sadness in her lovely wide eyes. She loves her mother, and I shall not be surprised if she foregoes marriage entirely to take care of her.

Beloved, if you should ever read this on maturity, I pray you, darlings, take care of your mother.

Our first, second, and third reaction was that our grandmother was unduly harsh on Daddy but raced through Mama's shortcomings, the neglect of her children being one of them. Buddie understood there was harm enough to go around, but she didn't perceive Mama's knack for bringing out the angry beast in all of us, not just in Daddy. Susan and I agreed that even if we'd come across the letter years earlier, it wouldn't have changed our life on Saulter Road, though Buddie's musings contained much truth.

When Buddie lived with us, she welcomed my sitting at the foot of her twin bed after school or on weekends, listening to tales from elf-world where everything was restored and lovely. Perhaps the happily-ever-after stories that capture our minds are a mere echo from another very real world. Buddie and Jadie Bell thought so, but my mind didn't focus on other realms outside of Buddie's tales which weren't true anyway.

Buddie suffered from high blood pressure, and the only treatment at the time was phenobarbital, which induced drowsiness. Thus, most of her days were spent in bed. However, at appointment time with her adored doctor, she rose to the occasion. "Hold my hands and walk to me," he instructed with a wink.

"Hold your hands, I'll do all day, but walk, I cannot do."

Buddie's legs ached constantly, and she seldom joined us in the kitchen. When she did, she stared through the backdoor window—her gown hiked with one hand rubbing her legs and hip, and a cigarette in the other hand, as she whistled little tunes.

At night, she left her bedroom only to plead, "Sax, please calm down. You're upsetting the children!" or "Elinor, you're only provoking him. Go to bed!" When they defied her orders, she stood between them, facing Daddy. Buddie assumed the role of nighttime buffer, at least for a while.

She was otherwise cheerful, but I learned much later that she bore her own shattered dreams, as evidenced in her poem, "Against the Storm".

> *A Joshua tree is one that is thwarted,*
> *Buffeted into a grotesque design;*
> *Its every growing desire is aborted*
> *I know the agony; that fate is mine.*

"When I get nostalgic or sad," Buddie said, "I like to go to the dime store and buy a little something." One day Mother drove her to the five-and-dime where she purchased twenty plastic angels, all a boring cream color, and her creativity kicked in. She bought paint, glitter, rhinestones, and colorful tiny stars to apply to their four-inch celestial bodies.

For hours, Buddie sat at the kitchen table transforming each angel. She painted the wings white, the halos gold, the hair and bodices silver, and each skirt a different pastel color. Then, with the precision of a watchmaker, she painted their eyebrows and lips and gave them rosy cheeks. Rhinestones adorned each halo; glitter and stars added the finishing touch to each skirt. Buddie presented her angels to Mother who strategically placed each one on our Christmas tree.

My beloved grandmother Buddie in 1944, three years before I was born.

We loved her creations because we loved their creator.

When Linda and Susan and I were grown and married, Mother gave us each five of Buddie's angels to adorn our own Christmas trees. Later, a fire destroyed all of mine. Gone forever! For forty-one Decembers, I missed her heavenly creations.

Buddie once recounted the evening when Mother and her brother Bill were young and, at the foot of their own grandmother, listening to classical music. Deeply moved, Bill remarked effusively, "Oh, MaaMaa, I'm just *full* of beautiful music!"

"Well, you must be, 'cause none's ever come out!" their grandmother quipped. Ironically, years later, music did pour forth from Bill, a radio host broadcasting and commenting on beautiful music. Bill inherited the musical gene; Mama, the wisecrack gene. For the most part, that gene didn't serve her well.

Addie Lee, our downstairs maid, had a similarly feisty friendship with Mama. When my sisters and I squabbled, Mama complained, "For crying out loud, these children are driving me crazy!"

"Yeah, and you ain't got far to go!" Addie Lee giggled, exposing her missing teeth.

"Touché," Mama said and chuckled back. We all got a kick out of Addie Lee's bantering.

We drove Mama crazy on other occasions too. "How many times do I have to tell you girls not to sit on beds when they're made up?" or "Quit rummaging around and messing up the kitchen!" If we upset her close to vacation time, Mama threatened with her lower teeth exposed, "Well, that settles it! I'm not taking ya'll to the beach this year." We saw an outburst coming whenever Mama jutted her jaw and brandished her bottom teeth.

"Please, Mama. We're sorry, we won't do it again. Please, take us." But regardless of our behavior, we never missed our spring and month-long summer trips to the beach. After several years, Linda, Susan, and I ignored her cries of wolf.

I was in fifth grade when it was Mama's turn to pick up carpool at Shades Cahaba Elementary one day. My friends and I waited and waited.

"Where's your mom?"

"She'll be here in a minute," I replied and prayed with the same passion I prayed in Mrs. Prince's third-grade classroom. I sat at my dark wooden desk with a hole for the inkwell and groove for my pencil. I recall the plaid dress I wore with a small white collar and can still hear my cry, "God, please make my mama stop drinking."

As the minutes passed at the now empty school grounds, I knew Mama was drunk. I darted by myself—I needed to be alone—to the office and phoned home. I let the phone ring until the sound woke her from an induced slumber.

"Mama, Mama, the riding group, the riding group! You're supposed to pick us up."

"I'm… I'm comin'," she slurred. Mother came, but *how* is a wonder of the first order. One glimpse of her bobbing head, scrunched brow, and stretched upper lip alerted me to sit beside her on the bench seat. As we turned onto Hollywood Boulevard right outside the school, Mama ran up a curb. There were startled gasps to my right and from the backseat.

Flushed, and with the rapid heartbeat of a hummingbird, I grabbed the steering wheel and became the co-driver, navigating the car all the way home while my five friends spoke not a word, their eyes as big and round as full moons.

The jig was up.

Five friends now knew what I'd heretofore hidden so well. The sky fell, and the earth cracked. Something in me died that day—a measure of dignity and worth. My two disparate worlds had collided and positioned me on a path of slowly succumbing to what Edna St. Vincent Millay referred to in

"Renascence" as a "flat" soul.

Even now, I long to return and rescue that little girl.

I didn't confront Mother the next day, and she never apologized. Our family didn't speak of such occurrences the day after—it was as if they'd never happened. Skirmish after skirmish, the pattern continued. We lived in no-man's-land, and we dared not peek out of the trench. I was the quiet, compliant middle child for whom "Peace at any price!" became my battle cry, and keeping the peace also meant never telling Daddy.

My mama. Some days after school, she offered me help on a school project, but on other days, I was ordered to get out of her way. We never knew which mother we'd come home to or which mother would show up next: Mary Poppins or Cruella de Vil. One had control, wit, and charm; the other was out of control, sarcastic, and mean.

We loved Mary but feared Cruella.

Television only added to my angst. Our family lived in the heyday of *Father Knows Best. When I grow up, I'll have a family like that*, I told myself. Little did I know, there are no families like that, and most problems cannot be solved in thirty minutes.

Could it be, I ask myself now, *that* Father Knows Best *did more harm than good?* On the other hand, was the show a gift to inspire families to strive for the ideal? Or was it merely entertainment? "On the other hand… there is no other hand," as Tevye concluded in *Fiddler on the Roof.*

Father Knows Best wasn't just entertainment to me. Week after week, it reminded me of possibilities beyond my reach, but we watched the show as a family which was a familiar comfort. Unfortunately, my parents weren't visibly inspired, though surely our yearnings were the same.

They were like porcupines on a cold winter's night. Longing for warmth, one would draw close to the other only to be hurt by the barbs. I detected the feeble and, more often than not, unreciprocated attempts. But there will always be Saturday, I told myself.

A day worth living for! Mama didn't drink on Saturday, and Daddy stayed home. Our yardman Fred came those days, and his presence and gentle demeanor had a congenial effect on Mother and Daddy's relationship as the three of them worked together outside. Fred wore a nice brimmed hat he removed only to wipe his brow or eat the homemade "meat-and-three" Mother prepared since Jadie Bell came only during the week. His good nature was contagious, and Mama doted on him.

On Saturday, Daddy set up either the badminton or croquet game, and we all played, including Fred. It was break time, and time-out for Fred meant making fond memories for my sisters and me. In the winter when it snowed, and yardwork was out of the question, Daddy and Fred hauled out sleds for all the children in the neighborhood to glide down our steep hill. Mother, Daddy, and Fred sledded too.

I couldn't imagine Saturdays without Fred, and I can't imagine childhood without Saturdays.

Pushovers when it came to animals, Mama and Daddy instilled in us a kindness toward little critters. Daddy banged two bright red cans together to inform the birds he'd resupplied seed on the squirrel-proof feeder he created for them. Once, Mama found an injured seagull on the beach and immediately carried the bird to the vet. Another time, she welcomed a visiting pet monkey and also nursed a bat back to health.

Many Easter mornings my sisters and I woke up to baby chicks, rabbits, or ducks that stayed on our heels and followed us everywhere. Stray dogs? Picked up and brought home. Mama especially preferred pathetic-looking curs in need of food or medical attention.

When our nasty mean cat (I have a scar to prove it) began to give birth, Mother gently placed her on my bed. "You girls come watch this miracle of birth!" Mama shouted. My eyes remained glued, despite the bloody sight. Afterward, the cat tidied up as best she could and licked her babies until clean and presentable.

Good mamas, I thought, *both she and the cat*. But why didn't Mama, who cared for animals, remember to pick up her children from school?

Down the street from us on Saulter Road lived a destitute family in a small shack, probably the first house built on the original dirt road. One night their home burned to the ground. The following day Mama said to me, "Joan, this family's lost everything. Why don't we take them clothes and money?" I emptied my piggy bank, and we delivered essentials to a grateful family.

Why didn't Mama, who cared for the less fortunate, abstain from Old Hickory whiskey long enough to gather us from school? Why didn't she attend PTA meetings where her daughters intended to show off their handiwork?

"What picture did you like best, Mama?" I asked innocently the first few times our school held open house for parents only. When she couldn't answer, I knew she hadn't been to my classroom. The American Legion across from the school served alcohol—an irresistible attraction throughout our grammar school years.

Why couldn't I attend camp or join the Girl Scouts? Not knowing the answers, I wondered if I was to blame. Maybe if I changed, she would too. Later, I probed for selfish motives. Maybe she didn't want to fool with me, just like she didn't bother securing letters and sorority recommendations when I transferred from Sullins College in Virginia to the University of Alabama. She assured me they weren't necessary, and I believed her.

Why did grammar school teachers tempt children to lie every Monday morning? "Who went to church yesterday? Hold up your hands." Happy and proud when I could wave my hand, I lied at other times but not completely. Some Sundays we started out for church, only to turn around and head back home when sober-mom said something snippy under her breath. Mother came to the car already a tad torqued because Daddy always blamed her when one of us girls couldn't find our chapel cap.

Why couldn't Daddy overlook one snide mumble for our sakes? Because they were gripped in their own struggle, words were their weapons. Unwilling to ignore her and now deep into an argument—an argument that made his face red and often brought tears to his eyes—Daddy would declare, "I can't go to church now!"

Looking back, maybe the only "church people" he knew gave the impression of having it all together. We were all hypocrites, but instead of hobbling on into a sanctuary, we drove away, suppressing and hiding our pain from friends and family.

We had much to hide.

In case an occasion arose when Daddy needed to protect his family, he hid a revolver out of reach in the top cabinet of his bathroom. "Do not ever touch my gun!" he commanded, and we girls obeyed. Psychologists term this "one trial learning" because Daddy never discussed the option of a decision-making process to help us decide for ourselves whether or not we would touch or play with his gun. No—we were never, ever to touch it, and we didn't.

One ominous night Daddy left to attend a city council meeting. After an hour or so, we heard Mother scream and wail as she scrambled to the bathroom.

"I'm going to kill myself!" she shouted from inside.

Susan, five years old and too young to grasp the gravity of the moment, merely seemed perplexed, but I was ten and Linda was fifteen.

When Mother locked herself in the bathroom with Daddy's loaded gun, her threat became a matter of life or death to Linda and me. Frantically, we wrestled to open the two bathroom doors. Linda ran to one door, and I raced to the other, crying and yelling, "Please, Mama, don't. Stop! Let us in! Unlock the door! Please, Mama, don't!"

Then... *BAAAAAAANG*! Destabilizing noise. Soul-altering silence. It seemed like hours, but minutes later Mama exited unscathed, although she preferred that we think she was dead. I don't remember what happened next, but later Mama told Linda she'd purposefully dropped the bathroom scale to cause the deadly sound.

What *did* happen next? If I'm ever able to get close to a black hole deep within the universe where everything around it is violently sucked in, the memory might be there, or perhaps it rests safely in Pandora's box and should be left alone.

As always, we didn't tell Daddy. The conflicts between our father and mother when she was drinking were already terrifying enough without adding fuel to that fire. So we covered for Mama to keep the peace. Protecting her protected Daddy; protecting Daddy protected us.

On nights Daddy wasn't home, Linda and I tried to study, but here she'd come. The interrupter-mother was impossible to ignore. "Please, Mama, we're trying to do our homework."

"Don't give me your guff. I'll talk when I want to. If you don't like it, you can leave!"

Linda did leave. She escaped to the car with her books or to Addie Lee's house in north Birmingham to study and spend the night while I scouted out other places to finish my lessons. After Linda married and I was at college, Susan grabbed her car keys and disappeared until surely Mother would be asleep.

On many nights, unnumbed by Old Hickory, Mama had a dark, disturbing ritual in my bedroom. Moaning to the mirror while slathering Pond's Cold Cream all over her face, she repeated, "I hate myself. Oh, God, I hate myself!"

I hate you, too, I thought, unaware of the source of her sorrow. My sisters and I wouldn't learn why our mother loathed herself until we had our own children.

2

UNPREJUDICED
FOUNDATIONS

M<small>Y PARENTS DIDN'T HAVE A PREJUDICED BONE IN THEIR</small> bodies. That's not to say they liked everybody. They didn't, but it wasn't due to any bigotry on their part. Had they been inclined to snub anyone, they would have snubbed snobs.

The movie *Driving Miss Daisy* chronicles a twenty-five-year relationship between a Southern older woman named Daisy and Hoke, a chauffeur she rebuffs at every turn. After Daisy crashes her car, her son Boolie insists on employing the affable black man and instructs him to report to Daisy's house every day. Daisy's stubbornness and accusations were no match for Hoke's patience, and he won her heart. "Hoke," she admitted in the latter years, reaching for his hand, "you're my best friend."

Likewise, our father needed help. He employed two maids and a yardman, but their closeness to our family resembled Miss Daisy's and Hoke's friendship at the end of their lives.

My earliest memories are of Jadie Bell, not my mother. As childhood issues arose, I always sought Jadie Bell first. When I was five, Linda ripped in half my finished coloring book where I had stayed within all the lines. I wished I'd been big enough to tear Linda apart, but I ran to Jadie Bell for comfort. My sharing problems with Mama only added to hers, although I had no idea what her problems were.

Throughout my grammar school years, I never questioned why we had two maids, while all my friends had none or one, at the most. Though their skin color was different from ours, they were like kinfolk, part of the fabric of our lives.

Jadie Bell spent the days upstairs cleaning house and preparing meals; whereas Addie Lee stayed downstairs, tending to the laundry for the five of us. Jadie Bell was overweight and built like a pear, but Addie Lee looked like a walking stick with long, gangly arms. The two were similar only in the way they wore their graying hair: parted down the middle with each side wrapped in a braided circle and pinned behind their ears.

Although Addie Lee appeared frail, she could pile our family's dirty clothes in the middle of a sheet, tie the corners in a knot lickety-split, and signal me to kick that laundry down the steps. After tumbling to the basement, the otherwise playful ball transformed into a mountain of washing, starching, drying, and ironing for Addie Lee.

"Now, go on and get outta my way!" she fussed with a twinkle in her eye, as she hurried down to the laundry and her stash of snuff.

White aprons covered their light gray dresses. "Jadie Bell, do you and Addie Lee have to buy your own uniforms?"

"No, Bodie," she answered using her nickname for me, "your daddy buys our outfits, and he pays my doctor bills, but don't tell Addie Lee." I suspected he paid Addie Lee's too.

Even as a six-year-old, I noticed Jadie Bell's poverty: the stark contrast between her house and ours grew more evident when Daddy and I—just the two of us—drove her home. The paint flaked on her little house that sat close to the road. It had no yard to speak of, looking like all the other homes lined along the dark street.

Addie Lee, long after she retired.

A young Jadie Bell on our front steps on Saulter Road.

"Lord willing, I'll see you another day," she said each night before closing the car door. Then I heard two of the four wooden steps leading up to her house creak as she climbed them.

Jadie Bell stayed with us the nights Mother and Daddy went to the Thomas Jefferson Hotel to trip the light fantastic, though they both had two left feet and never got outside the box step. Dressed to the nines, Mama added Toujours Moi as the finishing touch. The fragrance lingered and became my favorite perfume.

At bedtime on the nights our parents went dancing, Jadie Bell slept at the bottom of my twin bed sideways, on three measly feet of mattress. She could have found better places to sleep with my parents' blessing, but Jadie Bell chose close proximity to me, even at the expense of her own comfort. I never heard her complain.

Fortunately for Jadie Bell, my parents' nights on the town became fewer and fewer as the years passed. Once Daddy entered politics, he worried that being seen carrying his intoxicated wife out of the TJ Hotel would be bad for public relations.

Jadie Bell's home life wasn't without its own turmoil, Mama told us. Rearing two daughters and five strapping boys with a lackadaisical father was difficult (Daddy helped spring one of her sons out of jail), but why she kept going from her troubled household to ours remains a mystery to me. In light of the way she guarded and nurtured us, I believe like Kermit the frog, she heard the "sweet sound" calling her name to be our buffer, even before I knew we needed one.

I was born in 1947 during segregation and reared in Homewood, Alabama, a city adjacent to Birmingham. In the 1950s and '60s, I couldn't go to a movie, ride a bus, or use a water fountain or bathroom without noticing racial discrimination. We rode in the front seats; they were relegated to the back. Our fountains sparkled in the light; theirs were farther away in the shadows. Our bathrooms were accessible and inviting; theirs were not.

Fifty dynamite explosions between 1947 and 1965 earned Birmingham the nickname "Bombingham" during the Civil

Rights Movement. The caption "Bombingham" splashed across the front of *Life* magazine when I was a teenager, although I knew precious little about what was happening over the mountain on the other side of the soaring statue of Vulcan, overlooking and facing the city with his bare bottom mooning Homewood.

The cruelty of racial bias I observed was closer to home.

One summer while vacationing in Panama City Beach, Florida, after my eighth birthday, Jadie Bell spoke, as she had many times in the past, of her wish to ride in a glass-bottom boat, a three-hour trip away in Silver Springs. Knowing Jadie Bell's desire to have this adventure scratched off her bucket list, Mama announced, "Well, all right then, we'll go tomorrow!" If nature were inclined to join in a person's joy, waves might have clapped louder and stars twinkled brighter that night for Jadie Bell.

Early the next morning my sisters and I piled in the car with Mama and Jadie Bell to gaze at the wonders and fishes of the deep.

Anticipation heightening, we finally arrived only to hear, "Sorry, no colored people allowed." Jadie Bell stepped back.

"We drove for hours to bring her here," Mama pleaded, hoping to arouse a smidgeon of sympathy, but to no avail. Then she played her last card. "If Jadie can't go, none of us goes!" she asserted with the fierceness of a bantam rooster protecting her young.

After a prolonged and agonizing silence between Mother and the ticket agent, Jadie Bell stepped up and insisted we ride without her. Mama struggled with the standoff, but after glancing at us girls, she motioned us onto the boat.

Later, after the boat docked, we spotted Jadie Bell feeding nuts she purchased to the squirrels gathered around her. "I enjoyed these little critters coming to eat and play at my feet," she said, smiling. Maybe, but Linda and I read this as one more disappointment, one more demoralizing experience. Even so, we believed what she said. Jadie Bell spoke the truth and somehow found joy in dark places.

Also, on our month-long trips, Jadie Bell wasn't allowed in the gulf at Panama City Beach, so Mama drove us to Mexico Beach, a designated area for colored people. There I watched Jadie Bell and other black adults and children romp in the gulf. Despite her station in life, she seemed to radiate a joy that was pure, sweet, and real, long before going to Mexico Beach and long before Martin Luther King Jr. shared his dream.

Even before Dr. King aroused the conscience of America, my father supported his message. One of his best friends, a black man named Afton Lee, gained the respect of all who knew him. As owner of Afton Lee Grocery in the black neighborhood of Rosedale, Mr. Lee consistently welcomed Susan and me whenever we tagged along with my dad to shop at Afton's grocery store. He served us potato chips while we sat around the pot belly stove chatting with his black friends.

Daddy wasn't alive to learn that two teenagers murdered the ninety-two-year-old Mr. Lee in his grocery store. Homewood mourned his death not only because of his reputation and contributions to the city but also because he was the first African American to serve on the Homewood City Council.

Like my father, Susan also had an African American friend. While in nursing school, Susan asked to invite classmate Selina Hitchcock for dinner, unthinkable in 1970. However, without an ounce of hesitation, Mother granted the invitation. Puffing on his pipe, his eyes darting left and right, Daddy peered over the rim of his glasses and shrugged. "Sure, what the hell!" Susan practiced what Daddy exhibited.

On my first trip to Panama City, Jadie Bell had swaddled and carried me in a vegetable basket normally used for toting tomatoes and peaches. *That's* when my parents met Hilda and Dot, renters in the beachfront apartment under ours. They were Mama's drinking buddies.

Dot did not walk; she waddled with her short, squatty body and plump, stumpy legs. Yet somehow she managed to emanate a genuine femininity with her bleached blonde hair and bright red lipstick and nail polish. Daddy preferred Hilda, even though she outweighed and towered over him. He gravitated to her gruff demeanor as they spoke of sports and politics.

Air conditioning was rare in the fifties, and the heat drove us outside to gather in front of Hilda and Dot's apartment or on their screen porch. The Gulf of Mexico's million-dollar breeze and soft, pearly white sand beckoned us all to return year after year. Inside, the smell of saltwater combined with the gulf breeze wafting through rusty window screens felt even better than the sound and result of the attic fan pulling in fresh air back in Homewood.

We built sand castles with Dot. After laying the foundation, she taught us the art of dripping just the right amount of sand and water between our fingers in just the right way to create a stately, but delicate castle fit for princesses. Then we repeated the process, adding a bridge to yet another castle. We were the princesses and the castles our homes, but by late afternoon, our domain washed away.

Daddy joined us on weekends and kept vigil for hours at the shore's edge—feet apart, arms crossed, pipe in mouth—as we frolicked in the gulf. "Never yell when you're at the beach," he preached. "If you scream, you'd better be in trouble!" Reared in Flushing, New York, and lifeguarding as a teenager on Fire Island, he had pulled way too many people out of the Atlantic.

Back home, our family often spent weekends at Hilda and Dot's home on the river. As night arrived and bedtime beckoned, I thought it odd when Hilda and Dot headed toward the same bedroom. Though I was too young to understand the significance, Mama and Daddy knew.

That my parents consistently modeled the acceptance of others, regardless of race or status or sexuality, garbed me. Though not perfectly, that model fits me like spandex.

Mama always wore her hair in pigtails at the beach. (From left) me, Susan, Mama, and Linda, 1950s.

With Daddy at Panama City Beach, 1950s.

3

THE PAST NEVER LETS GO

L IKE A NEON SIGN, MOTHER'S LAP SIGNALED "DON'T even think about it!" but Daddy's invited "There's a place here for you." Throughout grammar school, I crawled on his lap and feigned sleep. "You're just playing opossum, aren't you, Ponzie?" (Ponzie was his nickname for me.) Yep, it was true. With my eyes tightly closed, he carried me to bed, tucked me under the covers, and always with the same question, "Aren't you glad to have such a nice bed?"

A child isn't prone to be glad about a bed.

My father was the ninth of eleven children born to Alice and Charles Crommelin Lawrence in 1910. When Daddy turned eleven, his father died of pneumonia, placing the lion's share of the family's financial responsibilities on the older siblings' shoulders. Daddy helped by delivering newspapers. After being paid, he contributed a major portion of the modest salary to his mother and bought socks with the remainder.

Daddy experienced the Great Depression throughout his twenties and then served in World War II. Mother told stories about the Great Depression, especially in terms of the coffee, sugar, and gas rationing. A bitter song, *Brother, Can You Spare a Dime?* swept across the nation. Those years were cruel and affected almost everyone.

"Come look at this," Mama said, motioning to me one morning as I followed her to Daddy's dresser. She opened two drawers packed with socks, nothing but socks upon socks. After all those hard times, he determined never to be without socks—or nice beds—again, not if he could help it.

"The past never lets go, Joan." I didn't realize at the time that Mama's comment was not solely about my father and his socks.

Daddy's older brothers funded his college education at Stevens Institute of Technology. At the end of his sophomore year in 1932, Daddy received a letter from a family friend and mentor urging him to specialize in a particular area of engineering. In part, the letter said this:

> *The matter of manufactured weather is becoming extremely popular with the public. You are familiar with this phase of engineering in the results produced in many of our theaters, in both houses of Congress, in many clubs, and now it is so developed that cold trains from New York to Washington are treated for heat and additional humidity in winter and de-humidification and cooling in the summer... read and study everything possible pertaining to the subject.*

Manufactured weather! After graduation, Daddy acted on his mentor's advice by forming a partnership with Doug Palmer. Soon, Palmer and Lawrence, Inc., represented manufacturers and sold to mechanical contractors and industrial users in the heating and air conditioning business—and it continues to do so to this day.

About the time Daddy and Doug's business needed another hand on deck, Daisy Haynes took note as her high school typing and shorthand teacher announced that a little company in the area needed a secretary. Daisy, in her poodle skirt and bobby socks, set out to Palmer and Lawrence to apply for the job.

She had no idea yet how dear she would become to our family, but she knew the exact location of the office. As a young girl, Daisy had roller skated up and down the sidewalk in front of the little row house turned commercial property. Daddy hired Daisy on the spot and instructed her, "When my daughters or wife phone, put them through no matter what." Daisy continued working at Palmer and Lawrence for fifty-nine years and always put our calls straight through to Daddy.

As hard as our father worked, he made time to play with us, especially in Mother's absence. Otherwise, the friction between them diminished his playful side. Placing us on his shoulders when we were young (but old enough to remember), Daddy held our hands and galloped us around the living room where we saw our reflection in a large mirror hanging above the mantel.

"Come dance with me," Daddy invited each of us when we were five or six. We placed our feet on top of his and waltzed away to the music (learning only the box step). Later, he bought a giant doll we strapped to our own feet and we taught it how to waltz.

Dancing may have improved our coordination, which helped us master the skill of bicycling. Running beside us on the wobbly bicycle, our father assured us, "Don't worry, Daddy's gotcha!" When I turned ten, Daddy woke me at six o'clock every Sunday morning to ride bikes. We rode up and down Saulter Road on those happy early mornings for at least a year, just the two of us.

Weekday afternoons? Seldom pleasant. Daddy became a different person when met by his liquored-up wife. From Walt Disney to Oscar the Grouch.

On those afternoons, I sat on the edge of my bed next to a window facing the road and waited for Daddy. Even with Jadie Bell there, nothing seemed right until Daddy came home, although his homecoming often resulted in fierce clashes with Mama after we drove Jadie Bell home. If Mama was in the sauce, anticipation and dread were kindled together in me.

In either case, when his car pulled onto our steep driveway, I fluffed the bed so Mama wouldn't notice my imprint and rushed to meet my hero. "Daddy's home!"

"Hey, Ponzie!" he said as we hugged at the bottom or top of the basement stairs, depending on how quickly or slowly either of us moved.

Daddy once heard me throwing up in the middle of the night and came to sit on the bathtub beside me. "You'll be okay, Ponzie. It's Mother Nature's way of getting out all the bad stuff." My hero made me glad when I vomited again. I wanted to make the bad stuff go away.

On weekday mornings, Daddy put on a show—a delightful one-ring circus—to wake my sisters and me for school, although Linda was never amused. To the jazz of Dukes of Dixieland, he marched around the beds banging whatever he could find to bang, but it wasn't yet time to get up. Act two of his routine hadn't begun.

After marching, he cranked up the radio volume and sang along with songs that ruled the day: "Lollipop, oh lolli lolli, lollipop" and "What's-a matter you? Hey! Gotta no respect."

Next, bright-eyed and bushy-tailed, he poked his head around the door jamb and pretended to be strangled by one of his hands. Enthralled and giggling, I waited for the final call, not nearly so fun. Daddy grabbed a towel, came into the bedroom, and popped me with it. Ouch! The entertainment ended, and I hopped out of bed.

My father, a member of the Homewood City Council in the fifties, served as its president during the sixties.

VOTE FOR

SINCERE

ABLE

X-PERIENCED

L A W R E N C E

for PRESIDENT CITY COUNCIL

HOMEWOOD . . . Monday, September 19, 1960

Pd. Pol. Adv. by friends of Sax Lawrence

Daddy's campaign poster, 1960.

When Birmingham executed official steps to annex Homewood with Birmingham, Daddy and Afton Lee stood shoulder-to-shoulder to prevent the measure.

The drawn-out debate grew heated and divisive. On August 28, 1964, Geoff Smith with WAPI news spoke this following editorial regarding our diplomatic dad: "Two men always remained complete gentlemen in their dealings with WAPI news: Sax Lawrence and Henry V. Graham. There were others, of course, but these men particularly stood out as thoroughly decent individuals in their contacts with us. It's a shame that some of the others around them took their positions in the gutter and remained there."

Two years later, citizens rejected being gobbled up by Birmingham. Daddy regarded smaller, localized government as more responsive and in the citizens' best interest.

Our mother, also a citizen, might have thought otherwise since Daddy was not home many nights and wasn't always diplomatic when he was home. We were not pleasant toward Mother when she drank. She brought out the worst in us, and the revelation discouraged me that I could be so full of anger and disgust.

My sister and I shamefully benefited from Daddy's influential position on the council. While driving a weary Addie Lee home one afternoon when Linda was sixteen, the conversation among us came to a halt.

The flashing lights and siren of a police car demanded that Linda pull over. She rolled down her window as she eyeballed the looming policeman's approach, growing larger and larger with each dreadful step. "I don't have time for you now, Officer. I'm in a hurry to get her home," she said in her urgent voice and glanced back at a shaken Addie Lee.

Cowering in the backseat, Addie Lee cried, "Oh, Lawd, girl, don't talk to the *po*lice like that!" He took one gander at Linda's driver's license and forgave her offense.

Another incident happened six years later when the police protected me. Two officers caught my friend and me red-handed as they flashed their lights into our car and discovered the beer—two underage teenagers drinking the night away.

After checking out my driver's license, they chauffeured me home and stealthily dropped me at the bottom of our drive. Then they drove Brad Kirby to the police station. Although appropriately offended by this show of partiality, Brad's parents remained silent out of respect for Sax Lawrence—respect he had earned the old-fashioned way.

When Daddy received calls from citizens complaining about the garbage service, this hands-on, onsite servant arose at four the next morning to ride in one of the garbage trucks, investigating reported problems or concerns.

Another time, as friends and I cruised through downtown Homewood, one of the girls squealed, "Is that your dad in the back of that police car?"

"Sure is."

"Your dad's been arrested."

"No, he hasn't. He just likes riding with the police."

As I matured, I realized his intention was to serve the city he loved. Now, in hindsight, I believe his contributions to the city took a toll on our family.

In addition to politics, Daddy enjoyed working outside on Saturdays while horsing around with Fred. "Mr. Lawrence, just look at this yard. The swings, the slide, the hills, the brick and rock walls, the patios, the woods, the blueberry patch. My title should be changed from yardman to park manager."

No, it wasn't a park, but almost two acres of land was plenty enough space for Daddy to create a children's softball field. "If you build it, they will come." And they did. All the kids in the neighborhood played softball on Daddy's field. We killed his grass, but he didn't mind. There would be time enough for grass later.

Like Jadie Bell, Fred had our backs too. One particular Saturday, while he mowed the front yard and Daddy pulled weeds behind the house, my friend Glenda Trotter and I grew bored.

"You wanna go to the hill and throw water balloons at cars?" I goaded my mischievous friend. Together, Glenda and I spelled t-r-o-u-b-l-e. Off we scampered to the basement, grabbed a fistful of balloons, and hightailed it to the water hose.

What a rush, throwing water-filled balloons at passing cars. A few drivers blew their horns but most drove on, chalking it up to a childish prank, until *SCREEEEEEEECH*!

"Uh-oh!" We skedaddled into the woods far, far away.

"Where are those kids!" the driver shouted as he emerged from his car.

"I don't know," Fred calmly answered.

"Who are they, and where do they live?"

"I don't know, sir."

Approaching Fred, the driver yelled, "Those damn balloons splattered all over my wife!"

Baffled by his lack of response, the couple sped off, leaving Fred in the dust.

"I… I think the coast is clear," I whispered.

We sprang from the woods and listened as Fred narrated in a fatherly tone the havoc we caused, and Glenda and I realized our prank went south. Further shielding us, Fred kept the incident to himself. He was more than Miss Daisy's Hoke to me.

On those Saturday afternoons, Daddy and I hauled debris to a nasty landfill, miles away in Shannon. "Come on, Ponzie, if you want to go." I wanted to be with Daddy no matter where we went, so off we tromped to the truck and headed west. During those long drives, Daddy shared history lessons and passed along nuggets of timeless wisdom:

* Don't talk over people. Listen and ask questions.

* If you're part of a group or representing a group, say "we," not "I."

* It's always better to understate your position so you don't lose your credibility. Should you have ten points supporting your argument and one or two are weak, strike the weaker ones.

* People are busy. Put your main ideas in bullet form.

Daddy's fortuitous counsel proved invaluable when, at the age of thirty-five, I began my twenty-year involvement in statewide public policy. Years prior, at his suggestion, I had enrolled in a debate class and learned the importance of thorough research-ing. Throughout my engagement in state affairs, I reaped the benefits of Daddy's advice.

Daddy wrote me the second week of my freshman year at Sullins College, over five hundred miles from home on the two-lane highway. His note came in response to a phone con-versation when Daddy heard trepidation in my voice, and his letter followed posthaste. Although I have forgotten how I felt the night of our conversation fifty-four years ago, today when I read his words, I am still aware of *his* anguish as he struggled to reach out to me across the miles:

[Excerpted from letter]
September 18, 1965
Sat. 7:00 p.m.

Dearest Joan,

It was a short time ago that you called. It is your first weekend away, and I know full well the emptiness and possibly the fear that you feel. So much has piled upon you—so fast...

You are experiencing the loneliness that is natural at this period of transition. It will be short-lived, believe me. Change, in itself, is hard to handle. It is more difficult temporarily in strange surroundings with new faces.

On top of this, the classwork seems mountainous but only because of the concern, loneliness, and lack of a familiar face to share this time of uncertainty with you.

When you read this, you will have already taken a fresh look and bounced back.

I drift back to World War II. We were in the middle of the Atlantic—in a small ship that had no business trying to reach England. Nine straight days and nights of storm—each wave rolled our ship over on its side one degree short of "no-return."

We were losing ships—not from enemy subs but from storm damage and capsizing. It looked as though we did not have a chance to make it.

At 4 o'clock each morning I had to put our above-deck fuel tanks in shape for 24 hours' use. I always stood on deck at this time—held on tight—and faced toward the United States.

I tried to reach out and talk to your mother and baby Linda. I wanted them to know that I had lived through another day, another night, and that I loved them.

I prayed for one more opportunity to see them before we got ZAPPED.

With new strength, I went back to the job of keeping the ship moving ahead and staying right side up. So did 47 other men who felt just as I, but each would not let on—each kept it pent-up.

Well, we made it! This experience was followed by others, but we made it, just as you will make it. Your work will settle down and smooth out. Your classmates are experiencing the same feelings as you. You will share these feelings and become fast friends....

Joan, we make no demands on you as to making top grades. As I have said to you many times: do your best, have fun and stay well. We ask nothing more except keep faith and know that your family loves you with all our hearts.

Daddy

Just in case I didn't bounce back, he added this promising postscript:

We'll come see you in October or you come to us, whichever you wish.

The disparity between my father's and mother's attention and affection for me was baffling, and I zigged and zagged between my relationship with each one. But when circumstances brought forth Oscar the Grouch and Cruella de Vil simultaneously, all the zigging and zagging in the world didn't help.

4

ANOTHER BAD NIGHT AT
THE KITCHEN TABLE

"WHY DO YOU HAVE TO BE SO PERSNICKETY?" MAMA scowled. "You'll sit here till you eat, even if it's just a bite or two!" This scene played night after night. I refused to eat much of anything until age eleven, preferring instead to build castles out of mashed potatoes or take cover under the kitchen booth. Our rectangular table between two booths afforded Mother and me hiding places. She hid alcohol; I hid food.

I ate Cheerios for breakfast before the age of six, and when I grew older, bacon and eggs and toast. Dinner and lunch? Not so much. I didn't consciously decide not to eat, although it was something within my control. Maybe I wasn't hungry, but for whatever reason, I paid a price.

In my forties, I was diagnosed with full-blown premenopausal osteoporosis. "I think your bones never developed properly," the rheumatologist said.

"I suppose that makes sense. I was always thin and weighed only eighty-eight pounds at the onset of my first two pregnancies."

"Yes, well, that does explain it."

But when Jadie Bell served creamed chipped beef on toast, I wouldn't touch *or* play with it. Daddy, a Merchant Marine during WWII, had a different name for creamed beef on toast—shit on a shingle—and no way would I eat that! So I sat for hours and missed riding with Daddy to drive Jadie Bell home those nights.

My preschool friend Diane McCleskey lived across the street with her parents and grandparents, and she often invited me over for lunch. As much as I loved being with a family who didn't drink alcohol, blow cigarette smoke in my face, or cuss, I didn't eat much there either. I pushed the food around on my plate while spying the adults roll their eyes at each other. Though self-conscious, I returned to the McCleskeys' table only to scarf down homemade pound cake and enjoy pleasant conversation.

Diane was a tall oak; I, the little twig. Diane's mother said we looked like Mutt and Jeff straight out of the comic-strip series.

Inseparable, we held tea parties on a child-sized table in her yard and spent months building a tiny hut in their garden. The rickety shack wasn't much to look at, but her parents were proud and provided the tools and wood to create the ghastly eyesore in their front yard.

During the construction, Linda tried to intervene and take control. One day, tired of listening to Linda's orders, Diane yelled, "You're not the boss of me!"—a statement Linda wasn't accustomed to hearing. Linda determined early on, just as our grandmother Buddie wrote in her letter years later, that no one would "dominate her."

"Serves her right," Linda said a month later, grinning, when Diane plowed into a pine tree while playing tree tag in our yard and broke her arm. Pine is soft but not soft enough to forgive a blow like that.

Neither is a wooden Chinese checkers board soft, and Linda played me like a fiddle. Desperate to attract a neighborhood boy's attention one afternoon, Linda proposed, "Joan, I want

Miles to come over, so I'm gonna hit you over the head with this board, and then you pretend you're hurt."

She hit me all right, but because I was so puny, the wood broke through in the center, down over my head. Jagged edges pierced my neck as I howled and struggled to dislodge the game board. Miles rushed over, just as Linda planned, and the pair freed me from my albatross.

Throughout grammar school, I grumbled, "Oh, no, not again!" Instead of driving directly home after school, Mother sometimes stopped short, about five houses short. From there she paraded me down the driveway, up the steps, and into her friend Francine Jones's living room.

"Sit while I visit with Francine for a bit," Mama said, like everything would be okay, but I knew better. I chose the same familiar chair, allowed only to play with Francine's woven, colorful coasters, while they skirted to her kitchen table and drank until late afternoon. I began hating kitchen tables, but I liked Francine; she was kind to me.

Mother once asked her to hem one of my skirts, to which Francine replied, "Bring the skirt and Joan to my house." She taught me how to hem, an otherwise elusive skill that came in handy when I reared three daughters of my own.

On those afternoons waiting in Francine's living room, I sat on my high horse and fretted. Why I didn't ask to walk home to Jadie Bell is beyond recollection. After all, I'd wandered farther than five houses long before I started school. Instead, I stewed— another bad night at our kitchen table.

"Hold your shoulders up, Elinor! Relax your brow, Elinor!" Daddy would say.

When I was twelve years old, Mother's drinking forced me to step in as savior after I thought my sister had been poisoned.

We were convinced a crotchety old neighbor killed our cur dog Bodine. With Daddy gone and Mother on the phone, my sisters and I stayed beside Bodine, watching his agonizing death slowly unfold in our basement. Dying is hard and can take a long time. "Strychnine poisoning," the vet said after the autopsy.

Our family was devastated, and Bodine's death was horrific, but not as horrifying as the next night when Susan vomited. Had she been poisoned too?

With only my wobbly mother at home, I had no choice but to drive Susan to the nearest hospital. Once over the mountain near St. Vincent's Hospital, Susan and I lost all memory of the rest of that night. Why don't we remember? Is the memory swirling in the frenzied black hole or safely filed away in Pandora's box?

Daddy taught me how to steer a car as soon as I could sit on his lap and comprehend left from right. I learned to drive with Daddy beside me on Samford University's campus before the roads gave way to expansive buildings (destroying all our crawdad streams). Daddy's training enabled me to attempt Susan's rescue.

Forecasting, averting, hiding, and solving problems was my sisters' and my way of life. As long as I lived at home, if the front porch light was off when Daddy climbed the basement stairs after arriving home, he either murmured, "I feel like no one's expecting me," or, "Your mother's on the warpath again." So either Linda, Susan, or I remembered to turn on the light, affording him a few minutes of relief, hoping he wouldn't notice Mama's condition if the light shined. But he did.

One look at her demeanor and gait depressed and infuriated him. We were sad and angry, too, but Daddy expressed his in no uncertain terms. Instead of leaving the room or going to bed, Mother stayed in his face, and her presence and retorts intensified the conflict. Sometimes when he moved to the den, she followed behind trying to pick a fight just like "ole Jeb" on the television when I was five, and Daddy took the bait each time.

Many nights after Daddy tucked me in bed, Mama woke him up to start another fight. Maybe she wanted attention, even of the worse kind. Those nights I haven't forgotten, and I often cried myself to sleep.

When her warpath nights coincided with Christmas, we girls piled in the car with Daddy to ride around oohing and aahing at all the Christmas lights. Away from Mama, Daddy chose to be jovial, and we all acted and chatted as if nothing had occurred. Even the next day, it was as if it never happened.

On other warpath nights, weather permitting, Daddy and I retreated to the patio and gazed at the moon through his telescope—a diversion that transformed our thoughts to a more tranquil place. Susan, too young to moon-watch, sat in a lawn chair or stayed inside, and Linda was usually away from home, always in escape mode.

"Just look, Ponzie! We're so small compared to the universe," he gushed, trying to awaken cosmic amazement in me. I so adored my imperfect father that his hobbies—governmental affairs and moon-gazing—would one day become mine.

Decades later, when my interest in astronomy waxed, my husband purchased me a telescope in 1998. Backyard telescopes had made great strides by then; one could go to the moon and beyond. The Beehive and other aptly named star clusters were in our scope.

Turns out, the world is a teacher, not just a stage.

Along with the telescope, he bought Terence Dickinson's *NightWatch: A Practical Guide to Viewing the Universe*. By way of little sandboxes and a humble thimble, Dickinson illustrated the vastness of the heavens.

[Excerpted from book]

[A] child's sandbox serves as a model for the universe. There are about the same number of sand grains in a typical sandbox as there are stars in the Milky Way Galaxy....Only the nearest stars, those within a few thousand light years of the Sun, are visible as individuals. A thimbleful of sand from

the box would represent all the stars visible to the unaided eye on a dark night.

But the sandbox is just our galaxy, and ours is merely one of billions. Every human on Earth would need a sandbox to begin to approach a representation of the real universe, and even that would fall short by several billion sandboxes. Just counting the sandboxes—the galaxies in the known universe—at a rate of one per second, 24 hours a day, would take several human lifetimes.

For two decades, my family has continued its own tradition, initiated by Daddy many years ago. One of our sons-in-law brings the telescope on our family beach trip each year, sets it up, and delights in what he's discovered for all sixteen of us to see—my husband, three daughters, three sons-in-law, and eight grandchildren. He found Saturn with its rings. Stargazing is contagious.

"I wish I was a bird," I cried out one day to Great Aunt Amy, as she drove me to choir practice.

"You wish you were a bird? Why is that?"

"So I could fly away." *Not from you, Amy. I love you. I just want to fly away.* I looked forward to the times with my great aunt on Wednesdays; I enjoyed choir practice and the ice cream treats; and the voiced sigh was my childish attempt to open up to someone who loved me. She didn't ask another question as I hoped she would.

Still, she knew something was awry. Months earlier, when I was ten, Aunt Amy complained to Mother in front of me, "Elinor, Susan and Linda get attention, but Joan gets little to none!" I

*Aunt Amy, who would become
like a fairy godmother to me.*

*Me as a choir girl in front of
Aunt Amy's house in 1957.*

heard her make that same statement at least four times, but she didn't recognize my tendency to hang back in the shadows.

When my status with Mama didn't progress to Aunt Amy's satisfaction, she decided to stand in the gap. "I'm enrolling Joan in the children's choir at the Church of the Advent!" she informed Mother who seemed pleased.

The Advent was to Aunt Amy a second home, and much of her volunteer time was invested there. So much so that in 1960, she and her husband, Phil Hudson Neal, Sr., gave their own stone two-story Tudor home to the church to be the home to associate rectors and their families.

Later renamed Cathedral Church of the Advent, the structure is an ornate old cathedral with captivating stained-glass windows, each one telling a part of a bigger story. Every Wednesday for two years Aunt Amy shuttled me back and forth from practice. Years later, I would wonder what she did far from home in downtown Birmingham. I suppose she listened as a "sweet sound" called her name to attend to me.

The combined adult and children's choir processional followed the cross-bearer down the long, royal-red runner. The whole scene was majestic and regal. Just like my effusive uncle—"full of beautiful music," I wondered at the meaning of the words we sang. "Onward Christian soldiers, marching out to war…" *Home often seemed like a war zone all right, but how do I win the war? I know! Maybe if I find Mama's whiskey and throw it away, our home will be happy.*

As a choir girl, soaking in the grandeur of the sanctuary, I also decided why churches have extremely tall angled ceilings and arches. They're designed to lift one's eyes and thoughts to God. I raised my eyes but didn't know what to think of God or what he thought of me.

My playful four-foot-ten great aunt retained a storehouse of jokes. "You want to know why I have such terrible heartburn in my old age?" she asked rhetorically at lunch one day at the

Birmingham Country Club. "It's because of all the words I've eaten over the years!"

Aunt Amy did speak her mind, primarily on behalf of others, and lived to be eighty-eight—enough years to have a lot of words to swallow. She once scolded Mother for her inattention to my asthma, which was left untreated until adulthood. Mama's drinking trumped many of her motherly duties, and I wonder now if Daddy even knew I had asthma.

Linda recalled my suffering many asthma attacks, but I remember only three.

The first acute attack in early childhood forced me to sit up all night and clench the sides of the twin mattress to help draw my next breath. Merciful Linda kept watch over me that long night. Linda didn't wake Daddy, and waking Mother would likely have been fruitless, if not regrettable.

At the age of twelve, the second episode occurred while at the lake with a friend and her family. The distraught mother helped me into a hot shower, believing the steam would open my airway. Soothing me as she wiped my brow, she said, "There now. There now, that's better." And it was.

The last attack happened while on a sophomore high school trip. Lying in bed, I felt as if I were gasping for breath through a tiny but uncooperative straw while others slept silently nearby. I wheezed and struggled until morning broke and my airway passage opened; I could breathe again.

I'm glad I didn't know at the time that Great Aunt Amy and Buddie's sister died from asthma. I do know Mama wasn't concerned, nor did she take me to the doctor, even after the "distraught mother" phoned her from the lake to describe my flare-up.

As I approached junior high in the late 1950s, my eating habits continued. Exasperated, Mama hammered like a commercial, "Nobody likes a bone but a dog." After an effective pause, Cruella hurled, "And they bury it!"

Even Daddy chimed in, "Eat! Eat! Eat!" He promised me a hundred dollars when I reached one hundred pounds. At the time, I weighed in at eighty-four pounds and would soon stand five feet two and a half inches—taller than both my sisters, but shorter than Mama.

Junior high was bad enough without my mother reminding me how skinny I looked. I already had enough problems with girls who wore the popular clothes and shoes that didn't exist in my extra-small size. And then there was the hair! Mine was frizzy when the style was straight. It was the 1960s—Joan Baez and Cher were flagships for long silky hair, but on humid days, I looked like a blonde Little Orphan Annie.

Frail, I matured much later than all my girlfriends and didn't become a woman until the spring of ninth grade. On that day, I waited excitedly for Mother to pick me up from school so we could buy the essentials a girl needs when she becomes a woman. The excitement grew to concern when Mama didn't show up, and I figured she was under the influence.

Finally, Elizabeth Anderson, another one of Mama's drinking mates, came instead and was somewhat soused herself. *Oh, no. Not her! She's an accident waiting to happen!* More than a few times, after drinking with Mama at the kitchen table, Mrs. Anderson had careened her car off our driveway deep into the large gully and required a tow truck to haul it out.

"Hello," I managed to utter with a stiff upper lip, now understanding why Elizabeth Anderson came for me. First, Mother hadn't forgotten me. Second, Mother was intoxicated, unable to get me or anything I needed. *What would I do?* Linda couldn't help; she flew the coop when I was thirteen. With no other solution at my disposal, I called Daddy—another brush with death by embarrassment—to bring home the necessaries.

While becoming skilled at making predictions, I occasionally encountered grenades out of nowhere that blindsided me. Linda had eloped at the age of seventeen; Daddy was out of town; Susan slept in a nearby bedroom; and Mama left to visit Marge and Ted Hart.

Smarmy Ted with his bloodshot eyes thought himself a comic. "Joanie," he said frequently, "your parents bought you for a dollar-two-ninety-eight." It took me a while to realize there is no such amount as "a dollar-two-ninety-eight," and it took even longer to understand why their only child looked different from most children. Their son, Eddie, had his first drink before he was born; he was a fetal alcohol syndrome baby.

I knew Mama would come home plastered. Ted and Marge were drinking buddies, too, but General Sherman himself, who correctly said, "War is hell," couldn't have calculated what came next that late school night.

On the lookout at the age of fourteen, I sat by my bedroom window and waited. Ted brought Mother home, and they were alone in the driveway. I watched him take advantage of her condition as he scooted over to embrace and kiss my slumped mother.

I pounded on the window! After no response, I beat the pane until I rammed my hand through the glass. Hearing the shattering sound from inside his car, Ted immediately helped Mother up the front steps while I ran to the kitchen and seized a butcher knife. As Ted brought my beyond-inebriated mother into the house, I screamed, "Get out of here or I'll kill you!"

"Joanie, Joanie, don't get excited."

I held up the knife in ready position. "Come any closer and I'll kill you, I swear to God!" Ted let go of Mother, and as she fell on the living room floor, he left. Eyeing Mama in her black-and-white hound's-tooth-checked skirt and jacket, I lost account of the rest of that night. The memory joined others in the insatiable black hole.

I long to return and rescue that young girl, too, but like Daddy's trodden grass on the softball field, there would be time enough for that later.

Not remembering what happened after harrowing events is similar to a nightmare when you wake up before it ends. Your car drives off a cliff or someone holds a gun to your head, but then you immediately awaken. There's nothing else to remember.

The following day Mother examined the broken window (not my arm) and either put the facts together or called Ted for a debriefing. In either case, she asked me to tell Daddy a stray baseball broke the window—a plan I had already considered.

As a child, I pondered many questions. Why did Mother abuse alcohol? Why was Daddy gone so much? Did she drink because he was gone, or did he leave because she drank? Neither, I now understand. Guilt and shame were powerful forces that screamed, "Go, go! Stay busy!" or "Drink! Drink! Run! Run from the potential of the present in hopes it will allay the pain of the past." So they ran and hid much like Adam and Eve and everyone born after them, including me.

My own attempts to hide, cover up, and make peace were as futile as finding Mother's whiskey bottles. I scouted out her hiding places, found the whiskey, then poured it down the sink. I may as well have taken Daddy's money and thrown it away too because there was always more Old Hickory.

5

THREE SISTERS: BRANCHES FROM THE SAME VULNERABLE TREE

T HE DIFFERENCE IN THE WAY MY SISTERS AND I COPED with an unpredictable home life is easily illustrated by an incident at the beach. A man hooked a baby shark and placed it in a water-filled hole he dug in the sand. Susan and I stood off to the side while Linda ran around screaming, "Somebody, do something!" but onlookers were only interested in examining the flapping fish.

During the commotion, I lingered nearby unengaged with the shark, but Susan, without a word, left my side, walked quietly but deliberately through the crowd, picked up the shark, and tossed it back in the gulf where it swam out to safety.

That about summed us up.

The ultimate poster child for the terrible twos, Susan, when crossed, threw off her clothes and streaked naked through the woods toward the Huffstuttlers' house next door.

Mama sent Jadie Bell, Linda, or me to fetch her before anyone discovered the unclad child. In the midst of public tantrums, Mama reacted, "Whose child is that?" appalled by Susan's fits.

*With my sisters Linda (middle) and Susan (right)
in 1965 at our home on Saulter Road.*

You're funny, Mama, but you aren't fooling anybody.

But like she always said, "The boogeyman changed Susan forever." Outfoxed by the boogeyman, Susan bloomed into a happy but practical pixie, making the best of every situation with a wit so dry if one wasn't listening, one would surely miss a classic one-liner.

In contrast to Linda and me, Susan appeared unflappable. While Linda longed for liberation, I strived for structure, but Susan seemed serene.

"I could never depend on Mama," Susan said, "so I learned to focus on the good. When my teacher assigned an oral book report, Mama read me a chapter a day from *The Incredible Journey*. I remember our decorating pumpkins together on Halloween. We fastened grapes on the pumpkin for hair, squash for the ears, green beans for eyebrows, a carrot for a nose, marshmallows for eyes, and red peppers for lips."

Darling Susan, it didn't take much to make you happy, did it? I understand your focusing on the good. There were happy times, but did you forget the bad? Could five years between us have made that much difference?

Susan's early years were assuaged by the fact that her tiny cluster of playmates also had an alcoholic parent, making life less embarrassing for her to entertain friends "who understood and didn't judge." She frequently played with Mama's drinking chums' children.

But then came junior high and her circle of friends broadened, as did her humiliation. One day while I was away at college, Susan undertook a frontal assault. "Go to your room and close the doors!" she ordered our drunk mother, threatening her life if she came back out. This day was too important to take any risks. Today was Susan's turn to host cheerleading practice.

Mama resisted, but Susan refused to surrender.

Around and around they quarreled until Mama sneered with those bottom teeth projected, "Well, I'll just go in the attic!

How 'bout that?"

Susan called her bluff. "Great! Go to the attic."

"All right, I will."

"And don't come back down."

Shortly before the girls arrived, Linda came by and asked the whereabouts of our mother.

"She's in the attic. My friends are coming over. Don't bother her."

"Susan, it's a hundred degrees up there!"

"I don't care. Leave her alone. She's asleep."

Linda, then married and away from home for six years, hadn't forgotten life with Mama and left the house immediately. Susan acted cheerful, jumping outside and waving pompons with her friends, while our mother lay in the hot attic.

I longed to rescue Susan too.

Three years later, Susan's boyfriend and future husband, Billy Key, saw Mother for the first time but not before having to step over Mama's friend, Elizabeth Anderson, crashed on the dining room floor.

Dumbfounded and alarmed, Billy asked, "Who's that?" with panic in his teenage voice.

"Oh, that's Elizabeth. Just step over her." Taking Susan's lead, he tried to disregard the passed-out body lying there, but soon time came for Daddy to arrive home from work, and Susan panicked too. "Billy, we have to get her home. Help me!"

Ignoring Mama as she lay bombed on the sofa, the two woke Elizabeth and assisted the stumbling woman to her car. Susan scooted into the driver's seat of Billy's car and followed behind through torrential rain to deposit Elizabeth to an unhappy husband. Rolling waves of water were up the Andersons' steps knocking at their front door. So were Susan and Billy.

Protecting Daddy from the spectacle of bodies on the floor, afternoon tow trucks, and a host of other scenarios seemed to us girls our mission in life.

*
**

"Mama, my stomach hurts. Can I stay home?" Susan asked one morning in high school.

"*Macht nichts* (it matters not)," she answered, displaying our German ancestry from the Weiss and von Mohring families. Susan elected to stay home.

Late that afternoon, Billy dropped by to visit Susan, who was really more tired than sick. When he rummaged (uh-oh) through the refrigerator for a snack, Mama was fit to be tied. We weren't allowed to mess around in her kitchen.

Despite the chaos within our home, Mama required that the house look pristine. Whether for her sake or Daddy's remains unclear, but one glimpse of my father's shipshape basement workshop cannot be discounted.

"Billy," Mama interrupted, "you need to go. Susan's sick."

"She looks fine to me."

Those were fightin' words to Mama. "I told you to go home!"

When he didn't leave immediately if not sooner, she grabbed a mayonnaise jar, held it high above her head, ready to strike Billy on his. At that moment, Daddy appeared behind Mama and jerked the jar from her hand. "Billy, I guess it's time for you to leave," he said, and Billy left.

During high school, Billy worked part-time at a gas station. As his and Susan's relationship grew more serious, Mother tried to torpedo their affection by referring to Billy as a "grease monkey."

"He's a pissant and a little turd of misery. If you marry him, you won't have money for toilet paper." Nonetheless, in the midst of finishing nursing school, Susan accepted Billy's marriage proposal.

"Mama, I can't stay," Susan said as she prepared to run out the door. "I have my premarital physical exam in twenty minutes."

"Nobody told me! Well, I guess I'll have to get dressed," our tight mother said in her Cruella voice.

"No, please don't. You've been drinking! The doctor's a brother of my friend in nursing school. Besides, you don't have on any makeup."

"Too bad. I'm going." Mama put on her tennis shoes, a dirty raincoat, and with matted hair, she stormed to the car. Her exposed legs were white and dry.

"Mama, you look like Columbo. Please don't embarrass me." Susan, already embarrassed enough by the thought of her first pelvic exam, braced herself twice that day: once for the procedure and another for Cruella. After a little run-in with the receptionist and doctor, Mother was asked to leave the exam room so the doctor could take care of Susan, his sister's friend.

Susan, the placid third child, then recalled scenes eerily familiar to mine, despite the age difference.

Susan married Billy Key at the Church of the Advent in 1972. Mama grew to love and appreciate Billy, a good husband, provider, and father. Curiously, he loved Mother and always gave her every benefit of the doubt, despite the fact that when inebriated, Mama had often phoned *his* mother to complain about *her* son. Mrs. Key, a forbearing lady, was rewarded for her kindness when Susan became the daughter-in-law every woman envies but seldom ever has.

Pragmatic and sweet to the bone, Susan captures attention when she speaks because when Susan has something to say, she slices right to the heart of the matter with what we Southerners call "good old horse sense."

Moreover, if one isn't attentive, one might miss her ice-breaking humor. We almost overlooked one of Susan's one-liners after Mother pestered her incessantly for nursing her youngest child Bobby for so long. Mama said, "You need to stop nursing him. He's gonna have permanent teeth by the time you quit!" Finally, during our month-long stay at the beach—where Linda *always* claimed the master suite—Susan caved in to Mama.

My five-year-old daughter Libby watched Susan nurse the boy who persisted, "Boobie! Boobie!"

"Whatcha doin'?" Libby asked.

"Oh, I'm nursing. But when I get back to Birmingham, I'm gonna wean this child."

"What does wean mean?"

"It means *wean* gon' do this no more!"

Like the bay leaf in soup, Susan adds flavor to life, but she was not unaffected by her childhood. Susan and Billy now live in the home of our youth, and the house on Saulter Road will always be home to her, for to this day as night closes in, "I still rush to turn on the front porch light," she said. "Not normal is it, Joan?"

"First, define *normal*," I replied.

Three years before his death, Daddy built a smaller dwelling on the property for Mama and him, and they rented an apartment until the house was move-in ready. One day during the building, Daddy was out of town, and neither Susan nor I could reach Mother by phone. As the day dragged on, we grew more and more concerned—concerned enough to drive to the apartment and see her parked car. We rang the bell again and again. Then we pounded on the door like jackhammers (and almost as loud).

Her worst drinking bouts were in that second-floor apartment, and I think Mama resented being moved from her home of forty-two years. Although she never admitted it, she showed it with sarcastic remarks and by cloistering herself with her whiskey, even though the long-range plan made sense to all concerned, including Mama. Daddy had her future in mind—she would live next door to Susan and Billy, and they would take care of her.

Of course, Susan and I suspected she was three sheets to the wind that day, but, still, one must look after one's mother. We went outside and threw rocks up toward the bedroom and den windows. When rocks became scarce, we removed our shoes and threw them at the windows.

After all attempts failed, we gave up. Daddy would be home soon to his tanked wife.

Susan and Billy purchased the original house and threw away the wretched kitchen table and booths, making my visits less melancholic. I'm glad she's there—I can't bear the thought of strangers occupying my childhood home. If strangers were there, I couldn't go back, and I often return.

The past? It never lets go.

"I know why Mama hated me. I've known it for years," Linda interrupted out of the blue to my family as we gathered around our dining room table for Easter lunch in 2014. Earnest, her third husband, flopped back in his chair and dropped his eyes. The rest of us stopped eating and looked up. I'd heard the story before.

"Mother resented me because they had to get married."

"No, Linda, that's not so," I said for the umpteenth time and hoped she would drop the subject.

"Just do the math, Joan. They married late in December of 1941, and I was born October 21 the next year."

"I'm not sure I understand your math," our daughter Katie said after mentally adding up the months.

"Just listen! January, February, March, April, June, July, September, October. Oh, yeah, they had to get married."

"You left out May and August," several spoke at once. Linda talked through the calendar again but still skipped May. When the omission was pointed out, she recited the months correctly and brushed it off.

"Whatever."

Her performance received mixed reviews. Some stared at one another, others laughed nervously, and one dear soul changed the subject. Throughout Linda's life, she truly believed Mama hated her, and her rationale, mathematics aside, was that Mama begrudged a shotgun wedding and her, in particular.

Therefore, in Linda's mind and conversations, the friction between them was Mother's problem. A problem existed, no doubt, but not because Mama hated her. Linda frustrated Mother to no end, and Mother was one of the few people to tell her no. Saying no to Linda was equivalent to saying you hated her. Add to that Mother's drinking, which didn't foster a warm, fuzzy feeling for any of us.

At war during the first few years of Linda's life, Daddy returned and admired his three-year-old daughter's strong will, spunk, and determination. "She's got moxie!" he repeated throughout his life.

In the 1950s, when televisions were coveted, Linda watched Daddy open the trunk of his car to grab a large box. "Oh, Daddy! Daddy, you bought me a TV," she squealed. With that, he closed the trunk and drove off to exchange the new radio he had just purchased for our first television set.

As Linda grew older, her moxie and penchant for life's trappings concerned Daddy, and he blamed himself for being absent during two of her formative years. As a result, he rarely denied her. *If only he'd put his guilt aside and broken the cycle early on…*

Linda's personality was magnetic to me. Whereas most of my friends were drawn to her flighty temperament, others were afraid of her. I loved shopping with Linda, watching her charge clothes and jewelry to Daddy with abandon.

Linda had the world on a string, but our Great Aunt Amy, the leveler, had a strong sense of justice and was troubled when she noticed Linda and I weren't treated the same. Sixteen-year-old Linda was gifted a brand new sporty car, yet when I turned sixteen, Daddy explained he regretted giving Linda a car and equated her failing grades and rebellion with too much freedom.

I was disappointed and wanted him to know it, so I wrote him a note three months after my birthday and included four used car ads in the envelope.

Daddy,

Please give me a chance to prove myself. I promise you'll be proud, and all of my friends would give me gas money. If you were to buy me a little used car by July, I'll work for you all August without pay. I'll come every day for at least 4½ hours. Please give me a chance, and if I prove to be a little liar, you can take the car away or anything else you want to take away.

Love you no matter what. Really!

Joan

I have no inkling what Daddy was going through at the time, but he didn't buy me a car. However, five years later, Daddy purchased Susan a car on her sixteenth birthday. I wasn't provided with wheels until my sophomore year at the University of Alabama. I used that old pea-green, smelly Chevrolet tank with no air conditioning as transportation to travel back and forth from school.

Mother wasn't afforded a college experience and yearned, perhaps vicariously, for Linda to attend Stephens College, a girls' school in Missouri. Mama's dream crumbled, however, when Linda failed at Shades Valley High School. Our parents enrolled her in the private Misses Howard's School for Girls in

Birmingham, but it didn't help Linda. Neither did it help when Mama called her "stupid" the few times she tried to lend Linda a hand with homework.

True, Linda wasn't studious, but she wasn't stupid either. She was artistic, graceful, entertaining, and brilliant at faking stupidity and passing off responsibilities to others. She eloped before graduating from high school but persuaded me to pretend to be her and take the GED test. She—no—I passed!

Linda confessed that she challenged authority and craved freedom at all cost. She cited an incident I remember all too well. When she was in her teens, Daddy had another phone line installed so she and Mama could both talk on the phone. "Hop off now," Daddy told Linda one afternoon.

"I will in a minute."

Five minutes later he came back to her bedroom and told her to hang up. When she snapped and called him a very, very bad name, Daddy yanked the phone out of the wall. "Say you're sorry," he demanded.

"You're sorry!"

"Say you're sorry, Linda!"

"You're sorry!"

With that, Daddy unbuckled his belt and spanked her with it. "Now! Say you're sorry."

Mama and I stood at the bedroom door. "Please, Linda, for God's sake, say you're sorry!" Mama begged.

"You're sorry, too, Mama!"

Daddy then struck her buttock with the buckle end of the belt and left the room. "I'll never do that again, Elinor. But if I were ever in a foxhole and needed someone to watch my back, I'd want it to be Linda. She never gives in. Even if the enemy took her prisoner, they'd never break her."

Three husbands tried but were unsuccessful.

I felt abandoned when Linda eloped with Sam Johnson at age seventeen. "Why did you leave and marry so young?" I asked throughout the years.

I noted her wistful tone. "I had to get away from Mama." She got away from Mama all right, but she carried unhealthy baggage with her.

Sam, the son of a prominent businessman, was deflated when his father said, "Son, if you're grown enough to marry, you're grown enough to be on your own and provide for her." Sam hoped his father would fund his college education until the two could get on their feet. Instead, he worked a bank job and returned each night to the trailer park and his new bride.

Free at last and away from Mama, Linda's lifestyle with Sam didn't seem to bother Linda one bit. She was hilarious, always ready for a good time or new adventure—housekeeping was a nuisance for another day. Rather than wash dishes, she hid crusted pots and pans under the sofa.

Linda's escape and newfound independence permitted other curious behavior. On pretty days, she left the trailer door open. One particularly nice day, down to one match to light her cigarette, she struck the final one and watched it accidentally land on a chair and start a flame. Right as she crouched to the fire for one last chance to light up the Marlboro firmly between her lips, Linda looked up and saw her refined father-in-law staring at the sight. Together, they put out the small blaze.

Unfettered and untamed, Linda had a hole in her soul to fill and continued to charge her wants to Daddy's accounts, a habit that infuriated Mama. "She's always accessorizing!" Once, out of spite, Mama charged a mink stole to Daddy "just to see if he would be as generous with me as he was with Linda." Daddy didn't make an issue of it since he knew his otherwise frugal wife was testing him.

When she was pregnant with her first child, Linda worked for Daddy at Palmer and Lawrence as a file clerk to augment Sam's income, but she had difficulty remembering the filing system and grew weary asking Daisy where this or that belonged. So, like with the crusted pots and pans, she hid files anywhere and everywhere, even dropping them behind cabinets.

As a result of Linda's filing solution, Palmer and Lawrence suffered a type of stroke. Unable to retrieve important information, everyone became frustrated with the mysteriously missing files, and all signs pointed to Linda. Daddy ended the mayhem by paying her a hefty sum to leave her employment with Palmer and Lawrence.

Linda and Daddy were like oil and water. To an irrational or obstinate person, my father would say, "Look, friend of mine…" But if one was irrational *and* obstinate, he called them a "pal of mine," which was far worse. Occasionally, he called Linda a "pal of mine."

Sadly, the world she held on a string became more and more fragile. After three children, Bo, Kim, and Aimee; a home in a desirable neighborhood; and thirteen years of marriage, Linda and Sam divorced.

She later married two alcoholics, one in 1976 and another in 1988. *Strange that she eloped in 1960 to run away from an alcoholic, only to choose coexistence with two more.*

Linda moved her children to a farm in Virginia with her second husband, George McKinnon. Surrounded with their dogs, cats, and goats; horses and a barn; and a parrot that flew from one side of the kitchen to the other, it was an active but unproductive farm.

The parrot's cage door stayed open at all times—nothing or no one should be constrained in Linda's world—and when it flew over us at the kitchen table, we quickly put our hand over our coffee mugs to avoid drinking feathers or whatever else the bird dropped.

George lavished Linda by installing a swimming pool and giving her children horses and saddles and trinkets by the score in order to mitigate the vacuum in his wife's heart—an emptiness that developed at age seven.

"I remember how happy we were as a family until you were about two years old," Linda told me on several occasions.

"That's when Mama started drinking, and nothing was ever the same again."

Linda's son Bo and George's relationship became a source of conflict in the new marriage. Linda believed Bo would be better off with his father and returned him to Birmingham several months after the wedding. Linda then sent the girls, ages fifteen and thirteen, to a boarding school. Although Kim and Aimee's father funded the girls' education, George continued to rant and rave about other expenses.

"Just pay everybody a little a month," Linda urged George, believing debts were a nuisance for another day. "Instant gratification takes too long," she often joked.

"I can't not pay der bills!" he growled, growing more and more combative, distancing himself from any fondness she ever had for him. I thought, *if only he'd said at the right time and in the right way, "Linda, we can't keep spending this way."*

When Linda and George separated, Daddy flew to Virginia to settle her in an apartment with six months paid rent. After Daddy's death in 1984, the marriage ended, but not before another parrot incident illustrative of Linda's unconventional life.

Linda noticed their parrot appeared to drag a small rug by its claw across the glassed-in porch. Flapping around, it seemed upset. Upon further inspection, Linda spotted the bird's claw tangled in the rug. Wrapping the balking parrot in the same rug, Linda took off to the vet.

After assessing the fettered parrot, the good-humored doctor instructed, "Nurse, hold my calls. I have to go perform my first rug-ectomy."

No day was the same, and no day was boring with Linda around. Moreover, she possessed a desire and uncanny ability to tell disastrous marital and personal stories and have everyone, including herself, in stitches. But when others attempted to share their stories, they only reminded Linda of a better one.

Married to her third husband in 1988 and living in a tiny country town in West Virginia, Linda didn't live within Earnest's income either. Earnest Browning had his own issues: diabetes he refused to manage, head trauma and severe ankle damage after falling from a tree in a drunken state, and a wife who didn't love or respect him. The constant verbal abuse they spewed at one another would make any sailor blush but her humor remained intact.

She often retreated to Birmingham to stay with my family, but on one occasion, our frisky dog—in the prime of his life—kept humping her leg. "Go ahead," she said looking at him with her hand on her hip, "everybody else does."

All the same, Linda stayed in the marriage. After twelve rancorous years, Earnest began buying all the groceries. Linda explained to Susan and me, "He has to go to the store because I can't steer the cart straight. I keep bumping into things." However, when the three of us went to TJMaxx, Linda steered the cart straight as an arrow. We pointed out that her duplicitous "slip" was showing, but she laughed and said, "Well, why should I do something for myself if somebody else will do it for me?"

We laughed, too, but shouldn't have. We should have defended Earnest and realized her philosophy was a portent of things to come.

Situated high on a hill overlooking the Potomac River, the older part of their house contained Civil War history. Bullets from the Union Army across the river in Maryland dimpled the brick foundation. It was rumored that Andrew Jackson had slept in the house, so Linda joined the Historical Society, but her involvement in that group and in the Daughters of the American Revolution and Colonial Dames of the Seventeenth Century waned during the next decade and then came to a crippling halt.

A mother's worst fear—when Linda was sixty-three, her son Bo died of esophageal cancer at the age of forty-four. In unspeakable grief, our broken-hearted sister understandably withdrew to her bedroom on the second floor of their house, a house that had been mortgaged and remortgaged several times for improvements and life's luxuries.

For weeks, Earnest, seven years her junior, climbed the stairs to bring her coffee and meals. Weeks turned into months, and months into years, yet he continued to provide Linda's every need. She left the bedroom only to go to the doctor or beauty parlor, but rallied each time Susan and I came to visit.

The three of us shopped, lunched, laughed, walked along the river, and enjoyed meals we prepared together. Susan and I understood Linda would never be the same after Bo's death, but we also knew she was capable of life out of her bedroom. Yet she preferred her new life, and after we left, she retreated to bed.

Earnest's health was failing fast, and he didn't know when or how to intervene, although I offered unsolicited suggestions. If only he'd said at the proper time and in the proper way, "No, Linda, you come down now and get your coffee and meals." Maybe if he'd said that, she wouldn't have become addicted to HSN and QVC—television shopping networks—and bankrupted them.

Lying in bed, she spent fourteen thousand dollars in three months. Hard as we tried, there was no reasoning with Earnest or Linda to stop the cycle. The more she shopped, the more he drank. The more he drank, the more our sister shopped.

Secluded in her room, Linda's COPD and lack of exercise took their toll. In 2008, she plunged into pulmonary distress and was intubated and on a ventilator for almost two weeks. During the first week, when Earnest told us the doctor was talking in terms of "putting her in a home," Susan and I drove the familiar twelve-hour trip and hurried inside the small hospital at four o'clock in the morning.

That's when we learned Earnest had never met the doctor. Earnest strolled in later the same morning, and we each introduced ourselves to the doctor for the first time. Susan's first priority? Get Linda off that ventilator, even if it required a tracheotomy, which it did. Her nursing skills kicked in, and her sweet demeanor and proactive questions played a pivotal role in the doctors' and nurses' attention.

"I knew she was somebody special and had a family somewhere," the intensive care nurse told us and Linda's two daughters. "I knew it as soon as I saw that perfect manicure and pedicure."

Susan and I came home after Linda was breathing on her own and the doctor had transferred her to a regular room. The night before we returned to Birmingham, Susan and I wound down with a glass of wine. This crisis was over.

I had no idea the constant pressure Susan bore until she began to cry. She'd been a stoic nurse for two weeks, pushing back against unhelpful advice and offering constructive alternatives. Mentally, Susan was on duty twenty-four-seven. Onsite, she and the doctors solved daily challenges. At last out of her nurse's role, she sobbed for ten minutes of blessed relief.

Susan and I continued to visit each year, and Linda rallied each time, despite the fact that a doctor had prescribed addictive fentanyl patches for leg pain. She came to Birmingham with us in 2012, and was by this time on oxygen most nights. Rotating shifts, Susan hosted her for two weeks, and I took the next two weeks. Her daughter, Kim, handled the next two weeks, continuing the rotation for five months.

During that time, I took a tumble and broke my tibia. Linda didn't notice or acknowledge my leg in a boot as I climbed to her bedroom on the second floor—step together, step together—taking on Earnest's role. Susan and Kim did, too, but Linda's youngest daughter, Aimee, worked full-time and couldn't assume his tasks. Besides, she knew better.

Aimee sought professional counseling two years prior after growing increasingly frustrated when she and her mom recounted different versions of the same events or painful memories.

"Every encounter with Mom was unsafe and tormenting," Aimee said, "and our conversations caused me to question my sanity. At last, a counselor affirmed me. I wasn't crazy after all. I just needed to learn healthy boundaries."

In the fall of 2012, after many forced outings and doctor visits, Susan and I drove Linda home to West Virginia in good shape and independent, but as soon as we entered the house, Linda headed for a hospital bed set up in the den. "No, please don't," Susan the nurse-sister pled. "Come sit at the table with us. Don't get back in that bed."

We kept her active, but Linda reverted to the familiar after we left. While she bought jewelry and clothes she rarely wore, Earnest, who worked from home, continued to hobble up and down the front steps each day to buy groceries and fast food. Otherwise, he lay on the downstairs sofa in dirty clothes, drinking day and night.

Housekeepers Babe and her husband, Mitch, regularly cleaned their home, but no one checked their work until Susan and I visited. "They aren't cleaning. They're just taking your money," we snitched, but Earnest and Linda didn't care.

Earnest's drinking had led his employer to offer him early retirement with benefits a year earlier. Unable to pay the mortgage for months, he filed bankruptcy and put their house on the market.

Susan and I drove to ready the house, but by now, after months of neglect, the task was daunting. We filled in paperwork to return HSN and QVC packages lying around unopened and worked until the house looked clean and presentable.

Unable to sell their home, combined with Linda's unwillingness to stop TV-shopping, Linda and Earnest were forced to abandon their home and planned to move their train wreck to Birmingham in the fall of 2013. That's when Susan and I grew nervous (actually, we panicked), even though we encouraged the move. They needed to be near family, but we witnessed a thousand ways how unnecessarily high maintenance they had become.

Babe did too. Babe and Mitch undertook all their packing and moving. On move-in day in Birmingham, Linda rallied again, dressed to the hilt, ordering Kim, Aimee, Susan, and me where this or that belonged.

Babe nodded toward Linda in amazement. "I can't believe it. It's a miracle!"

"What do you mean?" we asked, suspecting she'd discovered what we already knew.

"I've been working for them for over two years, and I've never seen your sister out of bed. Now, look. She has on makeup and is sashaying all over the place."

On the move itself, Earnest came behind, riding with the driver of one of two trucks filled with furniture and hundreds of boxes, many of which had to be stored. Standing on the porch, I watched as he struggled to walk, grasping and leaning on trees and cars in his path, while Mitch attempted to hold him upright. *If only he'd had the ankle surgery the doctor recommended, maybe he could walk.*

Boxes were stacked to the ceiling and filled all the space in one of the three bedrooms in their small, rented duplex. The rest was lined with Linda's clothes, creating paths from one room to the other.

Four months earlier, Susan and I foresaw the train wreck—no engineer, speeding down the track, headed straight toward us. We each had husbands, three children, grandchildren, and we were scared. Desperate to understand and accept our new role in Linda's life, we made an appointment with Wayne (Bill) Krug, a licensed clinical psychologist. After hearing our background story, Dr. Krug's advice made sense.

Before advising us, though, he related a personal experience. "I was called in by family and physicians because a young boy in Children's Hospital wasn't improving when he should have been home doing what little boys do.

"I sat and observed all that took place in the hospital room. When the child wanted water, for example, the nurses rushed to hand him water and held the cup as he drank. They did everything for him and created what we call 'learned helplessness.' I counseled them not to do for the boy what he could and should do for himself." Bingo! The boy was released a few days later.

Then Dr. Krug directed his attention to Susan and me. He advised—in no uncertain terms—"Do not do for Linda what she can do for herself. Furthermore, I'm going to teach you how to love your sister without being sucked into her vortex."

Dr. Krug suggested we make two calls before their move. First, Susan and I were to phone Linda and say we were willing to help if she stopped television shopping. We offered to pay for counseling.

Second, we were to talk to Earnest and tell him we were willing to help if he stopped drinking and went to the doctor. We offered to connect him with Alcoholics Anonymous.

They each understood and accepted the terms. Otherwise, the burden would fall on Linda's daughter Kim.

Earnest ambled to AA three times but never saw a doctor. After several weeks, Linda returned to bed and TV-shopping, while Earnest—clinging to door jambs, walls, rails, counters, and shopping carts—found a liquor store, establishing their old routines.

Susan and I heeded most of Dr. Krug's advice, although his suggested parameters required courage, resolve, and fearlessness on our part. Saying no to Linda for tasks she was capable of doing for herself conjured up images of yellow jackets swarming around my body. There would be pain—lots of pain.

Unhappy with our fresh approach, Linda recruited Kim, her beck-and-call girl who catered to her every wish, but Linda's demands increased, as did her grudges toward Susan and me. Kim had gone to counseling with us twice but couldn't bring herself to commit to the more loving plan. Little did Kim realize, she was committing herself to four years of servitude to the detriment of herself and her mom.

We missed the sister with whom we'd been so intimate. But now, Linda's propensities spiraled out of control, and her bitterness and lack of empathy for those who sacrificed for her triggered emotional alienation with those who loved her most.

When those outside the family didn't fall in line, Linda threatened to sue them. *If I had a nickel for every time...*

Susan and I continued to drive her to doctor appointments, while she drove herself to the beauty parlor. We went with her to dentists, pulmonologists, internists, a hematologist, an orthopedist, a sleep study, and once-a-month pain clinics for fentanyl patches.

"Linda," I implored, "if we don't get Earnest to the doctor, he's gonna die first." She didn't believe me, but one year after their move, Earnest died at home from a pulmonary embolism.

Susan and I accompanied Linda to the funeral home to sign papers and make arrangements, but Linda dodged the funeral director's offer to conduct a service by telling him she'd planned a private family gathering. The gathering never happened. After Earnest's cremation, there was no funeral, no burial, no announcement in the paper.

"Mrs. Browning, this is Erwin Decker from the funeral home. It's been over a month now, and we need you to come obtain your husband's remains. We've provided a box for you." After more weeks passed, Linda asked Susan to pick up Earnest's ashes and put them in the trunk of her car.

"No, Linda, I'm not going to get your husband, and I would never put him in my car trunk!" Then Linda asked me, but I refused in the same manner. Finally, Kim's boyfriend completed the task and stored Earnest's ashes in his garage.

Linda's shopping addiction and attempts to manipulate others stemmed, I believe, from the conviction that her mother didn't love her, and the death of her only son magnified her grief, leaving an even bigger hole to fill. Those reasons, combined with a father and husbands who wouldn't say no, plus the impact of an erratic alcoholic mother, had a profound effect on Linda and freed her to collapse in on herself.

We were three sisters, a branch from the same vulnerable tree, searching for ways to survive the strangling vine of our mother's alcoholism and the sadness it created. Susan fared better than Linda and I.

*At my daughter Katie's wedding reception with
Linda (middle) and Susan (right) in 1995.*

6

"I'LL SEE YOU ANOTHER DAY": LIFE WITHOUT JADIE BELL

Mama answered the phone early in the morning on my first day of seventh grade. I watched her walk to the kitchen sink, trailing the long yellow phone cord behind her. Then she kicked the cabinet door with her knee—a habit acquired to combat a sticky door that frequently popped open.

Mama's expression of shock caught my attention, and from her side of the conversation, I pieced together that Jadie Bell had died. Our fifty-seven-year-old protector had suffered a massive stroke after rushing to Iowa where her son Raymond lay hospitalized and near death. Previously, Jadie told Linda, "I pray I never outlive any of my children," and she didn't. A few days later Raymond died, and Mother and son were flown to Birmingham together for their combined funeral services.

After the news, Mama and I cried. Then she composed herself and drove me to school, and I did not protest. All that mattered was my stalwart friend and daytime savior was gone. I thought of Jadie Bell in every class, her kindness and loyalty throughout the years.

"Lord willing, I'll see you another day," was her parting goodbye each time Daddy and I drove her home. I pictured those gentle black hands shelling peas or stringing beans with the kitchen screen door slamming back and forth.

Religiously, Jadie Bell watched the soap opera *Search for Tomorrow*, mimicking the songs and words to all the commercials: "Brusha, brusha, brusha, get the new Ipana with a brand new flavor, it's dandy for your teeth." I pictured her wiggle as she sang the ditty, and I could hear her voice that day, a voice I would never hear again and would soon forget.

Only once had I remembered Jadie Bell in tears. I found her sitting and crying underneath the dogwood tree at the bottom of our front steps. "Oh, Jadie Bell! What's the matter?"

"Your mom hurt my feelings, Bodie, but it'll be all right," she said, as tears welled in my eyes. "No, no, don't you worry yourself about Jadie. Jesus takes care of me. I just need a minute." Less than a minute later, she scuttled back inside. I never learned what Mama said or did to hurt Jadie Bell, and if I'd asked, neither would have told me.

The day I learned of Jadie Bell's death, my mind drifted to our beach vacations in the two-bedroom upstairs apartment, paneled in pine throughout. Six of us shared one small bathroom, and since there were only two beds—one in each bedroom—Jadie Bell slept on a cot.

Each night she knelt beside that pitiful makeshift bed and prayed for us, tattered Bible before her. "Oh, Lord, please help Mr. Sax and Elinor. And help my babies Linda, Joan, and Susan. Be with them and let them be with me after we leave this world." During the day, I sensed Jadie Bell at the screen window watching us on the beach and hoped she enjoyed the breeze and aroma as much as I did.

All came to mind that long day when I was thirteen.

Mother, Daddy, and Linda attended Jadie Bell's funeral, but I wasn't included because I was "too young." *Why didn't I speak*

Jadie Bell and me at the beach with our
deep sea fishing catch, about 1951.

up? I was old enough to feel sorrow and loss and, most of all, pay respects to her family who respected and sacrificed for ours, wasn't I?

Had I been allowed to go to the funeral, I would have hugged Fox, another adult son of Jadie Bell's, who frequently drove Susan and me to Melrose, an ice cream shop, for milk shakes. Instead, I watched from the window as the three of them drove away. My bedroom window was so often associated with sadness.

After Jadie Bell's death, three things happened simultaneously and straightaway. First, as a fledgling cook, Mama's meals were sub-par. Avoiding hurt feelings, Daddy threw portions of his meal out a window at the end of the kitchen booth whenever Mama looked away. He motioned us girls to throw ours out too.

A quick study, Mama rose to the occasion, and her skills soon improved. After all, she knew all the goings-on in her kitchen, including Jadie Bell's recipes.

However, not many people, including professional chefs, after having one too many, could place chicken in hot oil in a cast iron skillet, go lie down, and listen for the sounds of perfectly fried chicken. But Mama could. Throughout the years, she branched out by preparing lobster tails, vichyssoise, and she-crab soup (with sherry, of course).

Mother went to great lengths at Thanksgiving. One such holiday, after my sisters and I had children of our own, Mama set a beautiful table and cooked all day. Then she rewarded herself for all that hard work by taking a nip or four before the families arrived.

The grandchildren took no notice, and the sons-in-law bore it in stride. But her condition cast an oppressive pall over Daddy, Linda, Susan, and me—a veil so thick a turkey carver couldn't begin to cut through our sour taste and disappointment. As we eyed one another, we truly felt the other's pain.

Daddy placed a child's card table in the dining room for the toddlers, who were served first. Tension mounting, Mama went to the kitchen for one last dish to bring to the grown-up table.

Meanwhile, our three-year-old balked at the food set before her. "Eat that, Katie," I said. "That's rude!"

"But, Mama," she whimpered, "I don't like rude!"

On the heels of a moment of levity, Mama tripped in, and the creamy green bean casserole went airborne before splashing on the floor, lovely table, and two unfortunate people in the wrong place at the wrong time, leaving a huge mess to clean up.

Our tripping Mama, who bred gloom like the Grim Reaper, had spoiled the day in which to give thanks.

In Jadie Bell's absence, we also lacked our buffer and go-to person after school, and Daddy's coming home every afternoon was now even more of a mixed blessing. The nights were often hard to bear. Once Mama and Daddy's arguments ended, I cried myself to sleep.

Sober but hungover the next morning, Mama cooked a hearty breakfast before we rushed off to school, but Linda wasn't keen on breakfast food. During the summer months, she often requested fried shrimp for breakfast, and although Jadie Bell had a house to clean and beds to change, she stopped long enough to cook fried shrimp for Linda.

Jadie Bell had been a trooper and loved us as her own. She answered the phone one day to hear, "This is Mrs. Reeves calling from Shades Cahaba Elementary. Linda injured her leg on the playground and needs to be picked up."

"Mrs. Lawrence is unavailable," Jadie Bell replied, "and Mr. Lawrence is out of town, but I'll come get her. Just give me twenty minutes." Mr. Lawrence was indeed out of town, but Mrs. Lawrence was more than unavailable. Mrs. Lawrence was smashed. Jadie Bell walked to the school and carried Linda home, a mile each way.

Three weeks after Jadie Bell's death, my English teacher, Mrs. Wright, assigned the class an essay. I wrote with ease about Jadie Bell and ended with, "I hope I'll see you another day…"

As a scrawny and unathletic child, I was usually last to be chosen to participate in sports on the playground. The daily rejection eclipsed my self-respect, but that was about to change.

Holding some thirty essays in her hands, our silver-haired instructor announced, "Class, stop what you're doing and listen. I want everyone to hear this." To my surprise, Mrs. Wright read my tribute to Jadie Bell, and the affirmation she heaped on me made up for all my playground experiences.

Classmate and best friend Jane Plummer sat among those who heard my homage. She knew and loved Jadie Bell too. Little did I know, a whole new world existed behind our house on a road parallel to Saulter, which I discovered only after my sole friend Diane moved to New Orleans when I was in second grade. Wellington Road lodged more playmates than a child's imagination could fathom.

"I saw a little girl about your age in her yard," Mrs. Plummer told Jane. "Why don't you go down the hill and introduce your-self?" That's all it took. Jane and I bonded when I was seven and remain friends to this day.

Daniel, her slightly older brother, broadened my interests and horizons even more since I only had sisters, but some-times he struck us with his knuckle and made bruises on our arms. Still, I preferred his attention over the soul-bruising at home. Although he pestered Jane and me, Daniel made life exciting as we cavorted with him and his friends, playing hide-and-seek and pranks on neighbors. The Wellington Road boys swarmed down and brought even more friends to play on Daddy's baseball field.

Hanging out with Daniel also resupplied me with a much-needed shot in the arm—hilarity and laughter. "What in the world are you gonna do with those?" Jane and I quizzed him when he slipped into her bedroom one day with matches. Turns out, he wanted to share what happened when he passed gas and struck a match at his rear end at the same time. What a burst of light! Many years later when I shot a .44 Magnum, I thought of him when the flash came out of that barrel.

Soon after we met in the second grade, Jane asked me to spend the night, but I still wet the bed. (I wet the bed until eighth grade. Go figure.) *I know! I'll not drink anything, stay awake as long as I can, then go to the bathroom very late.* So I accepted the invitation and followed through with what proved to be my not-so-foolproof plan. I wet the bed anyway.

Able to hide my predicament from Jane, I assumed once Mrs. Plummer discovered the stained wet sheets, she wouldn't allow me to spend the night again or, worse yet, tell Jane. Neither happened. I was invited again and again, and I wet the bed again and again. I loved Jane and her mother. Their home served as my haven throughout grammar and high school, especially after Jadie Bell died when I was thirteen.

I'm certain Mrs. Plummer knew of Mother's drinking problem. After all, Jane and Daniel were in the car that humiliating day in fifth grade when I steered the car home.

When sick, I sometimes stayed with Mrs. Plummer, and she nursed me back to health. Did she hear a "sweet sound" calling her name? She must have, since few mothers at the time would permit their children to be best friends with someone whose mother was an alcoholic.

Mrs. Plummer searched the *TV Guide* when we were young and made sure Jane and I didn't miss any of the happily-ever-after Shirley Temple movies. She drove us to the pool throughout the summer and provided the structure I sought. Mrs. Plummer played a major role in my life, augmenting those early years.

But childhood, even at its best, is as brief and breathtaking as a shooting star. "Once you pass its borders, you can ne're return again." Packed with pathos, the song "Toyland" is not unlike Mama's spot-on description of Christmas. "When it's over, it's the *overest* thing there ever was."

While I have no desire to travel back to childhood, I studied Mrs. Plummer down to minute details and filed the memories away for future reference. I wanted to know how normal mothers reacted in this or that circumstance, what mothers were supposed to say or not say in this or that situation. I studied the way she parented, the way she went about her day, and although it seems silly now, even the way she drove and put money in her wallet. I wanted to grow up to be like her.

At seven o'clock every evening, Mr. and Mrs. Plummer stole away, cocktail in hand, to visit. Their children viewed their parents' time together as normal, but what I observed was foreign to me. They adored one another. Jim Plummer once overheard his wife utter a whim, "Hmm, I wish I had a poinsettia to put right here." The next day, a poinsettia arrived from the florist with a card that read, "Your wish is my command. Love, Jim."

Much like Scarlett O'Hara, I swore with clenched teeth, "God as my witness, I'll have a marriage like this one day!"

In the meantime, I developed a greater sense of restlessness—anxious, easily startled, always waiting for the other shoe to drop.

Linda eloped the same month Jadie Bell died, and Jane and I started smoking. I was the bad influence, to be sure. Like Linda, I had a hole to fill, and an addiction was just the ticket. We bought cigarettes after school, walked to my house, climbed to the attic, and smoked until dinner. I inhaled before blowing the tension up in smoke and grew fond of the calming sensation nicotine delivered.

After each cigarette, we snuffed out the butts in my parents' wedding cake stored there. (Why the cake was in the attic, I don't know.) In any event, Mother never checked on us because our absence freed her to talk on the phone, drink without hiding, and smoke—just as we were doing—without interruption.

Each day, Jane and I finished our cigarettes before Daddy came home and in time for me to switch on the porch light and rush to my post at the window.

When not in the attic, I stalked Mother, trying to intercept her from her whiskey, even in the bathroom chest of drawers, another hiding place for booze. I morphed into a ruthless spy.

A shadow box displaying colonial spoons hung on the dining room wall, always at my disposal. If I stood in exactly the right spot, I caught Mama's reflection in the glass. When she sneaked a sip from her hiding place at the kitchen table, I rushed in, grabbed the whiskey, and threw it down the sink or toilet. She never scolded me or spoke of it the next day. Maybe she thought I had the moral upper hand, and I swung it every chance I got.

I missed Jadie Bell and wasted a lot of time trying to fix Mother, only to strain our relationship further. Now, when I place myself in her shoes, I resent me, too, but at the time, I believed flushing away the liquor would make all the bad stuff go away.

Life is brutal, with pockets of joy, respite, and beauty—a foretaste of things to come? Jadie Bell believed such moments were mere snippets of a future place.

I recently found this undated note Jadie Bell wrote. I can't help but wonder what prompted her desire to encourage me.

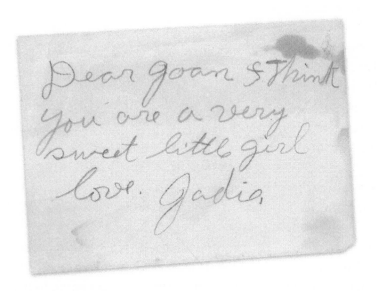

7

MOTHER BEING MOTHER

Mama conjured up fantastic descriptions of people that somehow made sense if one thought about them long and hard. Unless they were mean-spirited, I was enthralled by her shrewd use of metaphors, similes, and idioms. She sure had a way. "Yes, I see your point," she remarked to a pretentious but good-humored man, "but perhaps if you wear a hat, it won't show."

Mama didn't like Brad Kirby, my teenage friend with whom I'd been caught drinking. "Albino," she called him, mocking his fair skin, pale blond eyebrows and hair. Her perception of Brad changed one day after a tirade in the kitchen twenty feet from his stance in the living room.

"It's time for you to go home, Brad."

"But I just got here, Mrs. Lawrence."

"I told you to go home!"

When Brad dawdled, Mama threw pots and pans and tops of pots and pans at him, one at a time. But he dodged them all. "You missed me. Better try again!"

"All right, I will!" Another aluminum saucepan flew from the kitchen through the dining room heading straight toward her target.

"Oops, missed again," he taunted her. Within minutes, anger turned to laughter, and they ended up having a grand old time telling stories at the kitchen table.

Mother craved attention—attention she didn't receive from Daddy. Whenever I arrived home the least bit late with some boy she considered boring, she had placed a ticking alarm clock outside at the top of the porch steps to inform me I was late. On the other hand, if my date had charisma, she'd be perched outside, stone sober, under the dogwood tree waiting in anticipation for us to arrive. If he bantered with her and gave her the obeisance she longed for, he'd be invited to come sit at the wretched kitchen table.

My social life was full of turns and twists, dead ends, delights, and duds.

By my sophomore year in high school, I was still thin but curvy, up to a whopping eighty-six pounds, and never lacked for a date, thanks to my shapely figure and status in a good high school sorority. I never dated one boy exclusively until an engagement ring was on my finger.

Dating Charles Stephens all went swimmingly for months until the night he brought me home early and asked to come inside. Hesitantly, I agreed, but after a bit, Mother waltzed into the den high as a kite wearing one of Linda's old cocktail dresses. "Charles, me darlin', take me to The Club, and we'll go dancing." Charles and I blushed, and he left, never to be heard from again.

When I recounted this incident to Dr. Krug in 2014, at the first telling, he explained, "Joan, don't you get it? She was hitting on your date."

"No, I never thought of it in those terms. To me, she was Mother being Mother."

Mother being Mother. She called a person "me darlin'" only if tipsy. And if we flubbed, she'd say, "Amen, Brother Ben, shot at a rooster and killed a hen," or, with a little lilt in her voice,

"There's many a slip between the cup and the lip." In other words, mistakes didn't go unnoticed. Or if we had a hard go of it, she'd spout, "You'll be okay. You can get use to hangin', if you hang long enough."

Mother being Mother. "Joan Lawrence, please report to the office," a voice blared from the intercom in the middle of my high school world history class. I sped through the hallway, not knowing what crisis awaited.

Trying not to alarm me, the principal spoke words I never wanted to hear, "You need to go home immediately. Your sister called to say there's an emergency."

I raced home and up the basement stairs to find Linda nodding toward our pale mother lying on the dining room floor.

"I think she's dead," Linda diagnosed.

Feeling her pulse, I blurted, "She's not dead. She's dead drunk!"

We looked at each other and somehow found humor in the situation and got tickled. Having three sisters in the same domestic war often provided a little comedy for survival's sake, I guess.

Mother being Mother may be too dismissive a way of saying we girls had learned who to expect: charming Mary Poppins or unpredictable Cruella de Vil.

In either character, if Mama didn't have a drinking partner at the kitchen table when we came home from school, she'd either be asleep or in the kitchen booth on the phone with her colossal brown Aztec ashtray piled high with cigarette butts. I'd be relieved if she was sober and disappointed if she was tight. *I'll never be on the phone when my children come home from school*, I thought.

"I see your Mother's prepared us another cigarette salad," Daddy frequently reported.

In my junior year, Bill Burgess burst onto the scene and lightened the load. Bill, the funniest guy I knew in high school, adored Mother. She was crazy about him too. He was witty and bright like her, and after our dates, Bill and I often sat at the kitchen table while the two of them drank beer into the wee hours. Beer didn't affect Mama the way whiskey did, so I didn't mind.

Sometimes they discussed the implications of traveling faster than the speed of light. "Did you know, just think about it, if we could travel faster than the speed of light and had a telescope powerful enough, we could see Civil War battles or watch Abraham Lincoln give the Gettysburg Address?" Bill asked musingly and with excitement.

During their late-night philosophical discussions, I sometimes sauntered off to bed, but Daddy would awaken and ask Bill to leave, even though he got a kick out of Bill too. Once Bill phoned Mother at sunrise and insisted she go outside to see the "Big Eye." I credit Daddy and Bill with piquing my interest in astronomy.

Later that year, Jane and I sat in her new Ford Mustang at Burger-in-a-Hurry near the statue of Vulcan, and I saw a boy. If love at first sight held any truth, I was its victim. The most handsome boy I'd ever seen swept me off my feet. *He's the one!*

LG Cornell and I were introduced, and the feeling became mutual. After getting beyond his handsomeness and the notion of love at first sight, I discovered his sterling character and admired his ambition. The quintessential gentleman, he moved with the elegance of Cary Grant, and I fell in love for the first time.

After more than a year of dating, LG and I received a wedding invitation. The afternoon of the wedding, Francine, our neighbor five houses down the street, sat at the kitchen table with Mother. While Francine was a drinking companion, she wasn't without maternal instincts. It disturbed her, she told me years later, when I was a toddler and Mother placed me outside in an empty playpen, devoid of any toys.

"Elinor, she needs something to play with beside grass!"

"Don't worry about her. She's fine," Mama would say.

This day Francine said, "Show me what you're wearing tonight." Her interest genuine, I put on the old-lady-looking suit that hung on me, but it's what I planned to wear. Unlike my clotheshorse sister Linda, my selection was as slim as I was.

"No, no, this will never do. Elinor, we need to find something else for her to wear." Rummaging (uh-oh) through the closets and attic, Francine found an old white pique dress of Linda's, and although it fit me perfectly, it had yellowed and stained with age.

The youthful dress had narrow shoulder straps and fitted tight in the waist with a narrow belt out of the same material. It was low enough to reveal a slight cleavage and clung modestly to my small frame, not like the frumpy suit I'd settled for. A small matching jacket covered my chest.

Francine plonked down her glass, left Mother, sprinted to the washer, dryer, and ironing board, and got to work while Mama parked herself in the kitchen booth, indifferent to the impending transformation. Over an hour later, up the steps Francine marched to present me with the perfect dress. "Bibbidi-bobbi-di-boo!" A Cinderella moment, to be sure.

After the wedding reception, before going to dinner at Joe's Ranch House, I casually removed my jacket, and LG's look told me, "I could eat you up with a spoon." He barely took his eyes off me the rest of the evening, and I was grateful for Francine's selfless attention. She made me feel pretty for the first time.

"I want you to go to Sullins College. It's a girl's school in Virginia where you'll get a good education and make lots of new friends," Mother told me during my senior year of high school.

"Please don't make me go there! I've already been accepted to Alabama, Mama. The university's less than an hour away, and who knows how far away Sullins is? I can't leave LG."

"Just do this for me. Besides, someone better might come along. You might meet your fate."

Meet my fate? She's desperate to entice me. No, there is no one better than LG, and what is her fascination with girls' schools anyway?

"What if I get a terrible roommate? What if I don't like my suite mates? I'd be miserable."

"Just do this for me," she repeated, confirming my suspicion. Her own aspiration of attending a girls' school had been crushed many years ago, and I couldn't withhold whatever it was she was hungering for.

Mama's desire for me proved gut-wrenching, but since my parents agreed to invest their modest income on my education at a prestigious girls' college, I would go. Knowing my leaving LG was akin to leaving hope, Daddy pulled me aside. "If you want, you can transfer next year to the University of Alabama."

"Thank you, Daddy. That makes this so much easier."

Elated, Mama took me shopping and purchased clothes she probably envisioned taking to college had she been given the chance. We connected that day. She was giddy, and I was happy. Who wouldn't fancy hanging out with Mary Poppins for an entire day? We talked and laughed like girlfriends as we flitted about town before going home late in the afternoon to her happy husband. That was a good night.

When Mama was Mary, there was no one's company I enjoyed more. I just wish Miss Poppins had shown up more often.

Off I traveled that fall to a city where one could cross the line in the middle of main street and be in another state. Take your pick: Bristol, Virginia, or Bristol, Tennessee. Step right over!

My fears of a terrible roommate and suite mates disappeared quickly. Pam, Kathy, Rachel, and I shared the same interests and became a compatible, happy, fun-loving foursome.

Daddy wrote almost daily with a different gangster name or Italian name or French name or Spanish name above his company's return address. I anticipated who would write next: Al Capone, Gonzalez, Pierre, Willie Winkle, or a host of other characters.

"Daddy, you're so funny, but please don't feel like you need to write every day."

"I don't want you going to an empty mailbox, Ponzie."

His notes were short but worth the long walk down the hill to the school post office way too close to a foreboding slaughter-house. The woeful sounds of agitated cows woke us at six-thirty every Wednesday morning.

LG wrote several times a week and once drove a total of sixteen hours to visit me. I returned to Birmingham as often as possible to see him, and Daddy always purchased me a first-class plane ticket.

I flew home for a long weekend in October as Daddy had offered in his first letter. When I arrived at the gate, Mother and Daddy and LG were standing together to meet me, but they came in two separate cars. Faced with a forced-choice dilemma: Who would I ride home with? Who would I disappoint? I wanted to go with LG but chose to please my teary-eyed dad, although LG took it on the chin and followed behind to meet me at the house.

In December, compelled by a desire to be closer to LG, I told Daddy I wanted to transfer to the University of Alabama the next year. Daddy, the promise-keeper, completed the paperwork and the deal was done. There was no turning back now, unless I was willing to trouble my dad, which I wasn't.

However, the next month, my roommate Pam Atkinson arranged a blind date for me with a boy from her hometown of Greensboro, North Carolina. LG and I had agreed to date other people while I was far, far away.

We attended school each Saturday until noon, leaving little room for a robust social life. But as we came up from lunch those days, we peeked out the door to see dozens of boys wait-ing in the parlor.

This day my eyes fell on only one, and I thought he was fetching. He appeared entertained as he gripped a large black umbrella, leaned on it, and twirled it around and around. After spying on the boys, we girls continued up the stairs to change clothes. To my surprise and delight, when we entered the parlor, I met my date, the handsome blond umbrella-twirler! His name was Henry Kendall.

I liked him immediately, and his temperament was exactly what I needed—easy, relaxed, and not waiting for shoes to drop while I busied myself reading people's body language and facial expressions, wondering what their reaction might be.

Henry and his three friends had driven up from Greensboro and stayed in a motel near the college. There wasn't much to do in Bristol when boys were on a budget and still needed to have my three classmates and me back by an eleven o'clock curfew. So we purchased beer and went back to their room to party.

All went well until snow fell and covered the road in a matter of minutes. I worried they couldn't get us back in time with all that snow to plow through.

"You're a little uptight, aren't you?" Henry bellyached.

"Maybe, but in Alabama, a snow like this practically shuts down the city."

"Well, in North Carolina, it's no big deal."

"But we're in Virginia."

The tension on our first date didn't bode well. Otherwise, I enjoyed his lighthearted company, but he had no interest in dating me again because I was high-strung and didn't trust him to take care of me.

The next month, unbeknownst to Henry, we were set up for another date, but this time we enjoyed one another at a dance at the Bristol Armory. He was attentive and returned me by curfew without any prompting on my part. Little did I know one could be carefree and responsible at the same time. I thought, *how is that possible?*

I was responsible, studied hard, and made decent grades, but carefree I was not. Linda was carefree but not responsible. Daddy, Mother, and Susan toggled back and forth between the two traits. The combination in Henry was alluring, and I was swept off my feet again.

One Sunday, we rode in the country where we gazed at cows scattered across an expansive rolling field. "Watch this," Henry gloated as he let down his window and started to moo. At least fifteen cows came to the fence as close as they could gather near the car and said "moo" back. *What kind of guy is this who can beckon cows to come greet me?*

I was smitten beyond words, and our relationship developed slowly with mutual respect and affection. We built what I thought was a firm foundation—like our sand castles with Dot—except ours wouldn't wash away by morning. We could simply decorate with no guile or games or pretense. Loving Henry was easy.

Loving LG was intense, and we continued to write and go out when I came home. I dated both boys, but instead of being transparent as I had in the past, I chose to keep their knowledge of one another a secret. I had learned from my parents how to zig and zag between relationships. Moreover, in this case, geography was in my favor.

In the spring, my roommate Pam was to be presented as a debutante and invited me to Greensboro to attend all the parties and the ball. We were a middle-class family and lacked the money to buy the proper clothes and gowns befitting a week's worth of debutante festivities, but I wanted a taste of the enchanting experience, and Mother wanted it too.

At Sullins, I had been thrown into a world unlike mine. I had known it the instant I compared the contents of Pam's closet to mine. Her closet hung six fashionable Villager dresses to my one, and she used a gadget to place over her door to hang even more clothes; whereas all of mine fit nicely in one space with room to spare.

Mama enlisted my fairy godmother to fulfill our wishes. When I came home in March, Aunt Amy, Mama, and I shopped for three days at the best stores in Birmingham—Blach's and Burger-Phillips—and Aunt Amy footed the bill. We selected five dresses, two ball gowns, shoes, and jewelry to match.

Three wonderful days! I didn't fully understand her generosity or communicate adequately my appreciation at the time. There are no words, at least not in the English language, to express what I now feel about Aunt Amy taking me under her wing. Perhaps if I knew Greek, I could.

LG was unable to come to the ball, so I invited Frank, another boy I'd occasionally dated in Birmingham. Frank had already sent his suitcase ahead to Pam's home, but, by then, I was so taken with Henry, I asked him to escort me instead.

Pam drove me to the Western Union where I sent Frank a telegram saying my plans had changed. Imagine the shame and guilt I felt when I drove to his house back in Birmingham to return his suitcase, a suitcase full of clothes and expectations.

Totally self-absorbed and with a deflating soul, I had a ball with Henry. Now I loved two men, both three years older than I, although they were polar opposites. LG was formal; Henry was casual. LG's nature was serious; Henry's was jovial. LG had his future completely mapped out; Henry was content but held a strong work ethic.

When at Sullins, I wanted to fly home to LG, and after I transferred to the University of Alabama in Tuscaloosa, I wanted to fly to Henry in North Carolina. Daddy told me my romances were becoming expensive. Poor Daddy.

I flew to Greensboro every other month to see Henry and stayed with his family. He hitchhiked every other month to see me but settled in a motel. Once, when he was in town, Cruella appeared in a fit of rage, and I feared Henry would take another hike far from my family. Instead, he followed behind as I fled to the basement and wrapped me in his arms.

8

TIPPING POINT

═══════════════

HENRY PROPOSED DURING SPRING BREAK IN MYRTLE BEACH, South Carolina, shortly before I ended my sophomore year at the university. LG had proposed a month earlier, and now it was time to get off the dime, or I would lose them both.

I bolted to my unprejudiced dad. "I need your advice, Daddy. I love them both. I don't know which one to marry." He ushered me into the den and sat me at the same table where he'd tutored me in geometry five years earlier.

My father kept a six-inch ruler in his pocket and used it each time he corresponded or wrote proposals or signed his name. Everything had to be straight-edged to this engineer. If a picture in a waiting room was askew, Daddy straightened it.

After pulling out a yellow legal pad, he drew a ruler-straight line across the top and down the middle. Next, he drew a line across the middle of the page. Above the top line he wrote "Henry" on one side and "LG" on the other. Under each name he wrote "pros" and "cons."

The smoke from Daddy's pipe curled toward his widow's peak as he placed the pad in front of me. "Fill the page, Ponzie, and then we'll talk."

This exercise lasted longer than either of us anticipated and covered more than one page because it was paramount to be as thorough and objective as possible. Only then could my father guide me. I trusted his counsel because no one loved me more or knew better what I needed in a husband. This was my tipping point moment.

The project, once completed, didn't provide sufficient contrast for me at all. After taking the pages to Daddy, he studied them carefully. "I think I would go with Henry Covington Kendall." Those were his exact and only words.

Thrilling, but what had Daddy seen I had overlooked? I looked again after having had his one sentence input and noted that LG liked my nails manicured and pointed out the red marks on my heels from wearing loafers. (I suppose Mama's remarks about my appearance had groomed me to tolerate such nitpicky critiques.)

Once, I ironed a shirt for LG but gave less attention to the tucked-in part. No, that wouldn't do; he wanted it all starched and ironed the same. *No wonder he always looks so sharp,* I thought. He called one night and asked to come over. "Sure, but my hair's in rollers. Hope you don't mind." But he did mind and asked me to take them out before he came.

Significantly, LG declined my requests to meet his parents. Nor did he want me to meet his brother, his only sibling. Was he ashamed of *me*? Or was he ashamed of *them*?

I knew Henry's family well: his father, mother, three sisters, and younger brother by thirteen years. Going to their house reminded me of being at Diane's as a child, except there was laughter galore, no eyes rolled, and I wasn't self-conscious.

Henry was proud of his family and wanted me to be part of it. He accepted me, warts and all—unmanicured nails, red heels, curlers in hair—and he didn't scrutinize me.

Then I saw it as clear as day! Unconditional acceptance overruled all other scribblings on Daddy's legal pad that day.

And what was that other ever-so-subtle affirmation between those well-thought-out lines I couldn't quite put my finger on? *Think! Think!* Yes, there it is, Henry's a lot like my dad!

I reckon Mama could say I shot at a rooster and killed a rooster. She was right. I met my fate at Sullins College.

Thirteen years into the marriage, I mustered the gumption to ask Henry a non-straightforward question while on our way home with our three daughters from visiting Linda and George on their farm in northeast Virginia. The exit to Sullins lay ahead.

"Henry, I don't suppose you'd pull off in Bristol and let me show the girls where I went to school, would you?" My husband didn't deviate from his charted course when traveling, not one iota. He stopped only for gas, fast food, and rest stops. I've passed many attractive antique stores and flea markets while on the road with Henry, but marriage is full of give and take. For the most part, I take and Henry gives.

"I think that's a great idea. Sorry I didn't think of it." I was touched that Henry intuited how important returning to Sullins was to me.

We drove the steep hill to Martin Hall where Pam and I had signed in many nights at the desk beside the parlor before climbing the stairs to our room.

Eager to show our daughters, Katie, Meg, and Libby, where I first clapped eyes on their dad, like a mother duck, I led the crew inside the huge front doors to the parlor.

I rushed to the spot where Henry twirled his umbrella thirteen years earlier. "Your dad stood right here. Right here! The room was full of boys, but your dad caught my eye. Now, come see where I was." They followed me to the stairwell where I acted peeking out the door and seeing Henry before hustling up the stairs to change clothes.

"Aww, we wanna see your bedroom too!" Alas, they were in the moment. Excited and nostalgic, I led them to the second floor, second door on the right. Upon entering the empty room, no one spoke; we were taken back in time. Curious, they began to ask, "Where was your bed, Mama? Where was your desk? Which closet was yours?"

"My closet was here, right of Pam's, and this is where I placed my bed, which was right about here, next to the window," I told them as I reminisced about the fond memories made in that room. "Come look out the window. See way down there? That's where the post office used to be. I walked down and up that steep hill every day, rain or shine."

Then I cried and thanked Henry for including our girls on my trip down memory lane.

We meandered around campus, then hit the road. Two hours into the second leg of our trip, I was unusually quiet. "You're still at Sullins, aren't you?" Henry whispered.

"Yes, I am, but I'll be back. I just need a minute."

I was thinking of all the good times and the days I scooted to the post office, hoping to find a letter from Mama, but she wrote only three times. Nevertheless, I was glad that, in some small way, I fulfilled her castle in the air.

9

IRRESISTIBLE GRACE

Back when Henry and I became engaged, up shot the courtship costs. While happy to have Mother and Aunt Amy plan the wedding, I went toe-to-toe with Mama over who would be bridesmaids. She didn't approve one of my choices. "I can't abide her!" Mama chided.

As we locked horns, my eyes fixed on her prized marbled statue of *The Thinker* in a prominent place in the living room. Standing a foot tall, *The Thinker* himself didn't stand, mind you, but every fraction of his nude body was gripped in thought.

Real thinking isn't easy, according to its creator, Auguste Rodin, and I couldn't agree more. But I wasn't thinking straight the day of our argument because I interrupted *The Thinker's* reverie by hurling him across the living room floor, where he collapsed into dozens of pieces, beyond repair. It would be the first time I ever threw anything.

Clearly disappointed, Mother wasn't angry. My own display of fury alarmed her, and perhaps, at that moment, she understood an otherwise compliant bride should have a little say regarding her wedding.

Here's the rub: I decided not to include my friend Mother "couldn't abide" because I worried Mama might say something snide to her. Mama's prickly remarks often went over the target's head, but not mine.

As the wedding drew near, Aunt Amy and I went shopping again, and she purchased our living room furniture: a sofa, four tables, two chairs, two lamps, and a large antique map of the world. Then, as the crowning jewel, she bought me an elegant Lucie Ann peignoir set that resembled a wedding gown more than a nightgown.

In November of 1967, Daddy and I strolled arm-in-arm down the royal red runner at the Church of the Advent. Mother was gracious and exceeded my expectations by having the families to the house after the wedding reception. As I changed into my going-away suit, Mama came in and pecked me goodbye on my lips.

Unlike today's exotic honeymoons, Henry and I spent ours in Atlanta, and I could kick myself all over that city because I forgot to take the corsage pinned over our bed on the fifth floor of the new Regency Hyatt Hotel, now dwarfed by skyscrapers.

We moved to an apartment in Raleigh, North Carolina, and although Henry traveled during the week with Dayco Corporation, it was good to bond without family around. With no friends in Raleigh and on a tight budget, I worked as a bookkeeper in a small, windowless room and longed for the weekends. In the meantime, I taught myself how to cook.

The kitchen was off-limits for the most part when we were young, and we threw dirty clothes in the hamper only to find them washed and pressed, back where they belonged. I learned about the ever-present dust bunnies hiding under beds and in every corner and how to get rid of them. I needed tools, lots of tools.

I recalled Jadie Bell pushing an upright Hoover across the floor with itty-bitty me perched on the front as we laughed, and she glided me over the carpet. In light of that fun memory, I bought a Hoover vacuum first.

*With Daddy before he
walked me down the aisle.*

*Henry and I share
wedding cake.*

Early in the marriage, Henry and I purchased a boat that we hauled to a nearby lake. We made pallets with leaves and pine straw and laid out our sleeping bags. No tent for us; we slept under the stars! It was peaceful being married to Henry and very contrary to life on Saulter Road.

But I was not at peace. I was a new bride unable to leave my excessive anxiety at the altar simply because Daddy had given me away and I said, "I do." Henry, on the other hand, never gave the impression of being anxious or worried. He was a happy, adventurous chap and at no time brought work concerns home. On top of this, empathy came easy for him.

Soon after we married, Daddy called while we were eating tomato soup. I don't know what Henry heard or what I said, but when I hung up the phone, I saw tears in his eyes.

"Oh, Henry, what's the matter?"

"I'm homesick *for* you." *I'm glad I married you.*

Daddy was right and knew me like no other, even though I never crossed him. I watched Linda go up against Daddy and not once did it end well. Daddy never laid a hand on me, but I had anger all the same, even in the midst of a peaceful environment with Henry.

Alone, I threw something for the second time at our apartment on Carroll Drive in Raleigh. Every so often, Mother gave me useful advice, and in a moment of weakness, I phoned her for some tea and sympathy. Henry's traveling left me lonely, and I needed encouragement.

But how was I to know Cruella would answer the phone?

"That's the way marriage is. You'd better just get used to it!" she blasted.

Bad mother.

After soaking in her fatalistic advice, I slung a 78-rpm record at the closet leaving a long trail of black marks along the doors. Those unforgettable marks were still there in 1968 when Henry accepted a job in Birmingham, before going to work for my father four years later.

My anger would rear its nasty head again. Two years after we married, I received a phone call that my longtime friend— the boy I had been caught drinking with—Brad Kirby—died while serving in the Air Force and flying over Guam. The pilot suffered vertigo, and the bodies were never recovered from the North Pacific Ocean.

Our three-month-old daughter was in the midst of a crying spell when I learned of Brad's death. Both of us inconsolable, I tossed our baby Katie in her crib! It would be the third of four times I ever threw anything.

Otherwise, life was mostly serene. But why, when there was peace at last, did I lash out? Circumstantial peace and inner-peace, I learned, are vastly different. We were living in the Dewberry Garden Apartments in English Village in Birmingham when I threw something for the fourth and last time.

Katie lay in her pumpkin seat on the living room floor while Henry and I argued about who knows what. A pewter tea set Aunt Amy gave us sat harmlessly on a curio, and tiny Katie cooed, unaware of what her mother was about to inflict on her. Enraged and with the sweep of my angry arm, the pewter hurtled through the air and a piece struck Katie on her forehead.

Bad mother.

I expected to be shown the door right then and there. I deserved my marching orders. Instead, when Henry heard Katie's cry and knew she was okay, he spun and saw the horror on my face. He reached for *me*—held me tight, and we cried. Then we consoled our baby.

I have not thrown anything since that powerful experience of pure, unadulterated grace. Not a pencil, not even a cotton ball.

My behavior improved but not my disposition. I grew miserable and robotic, going through the motions and performing duties with an alienating attitude. My detachment and inability to love or be lovable caused a terrifying inadequacy and void.

Up until then, I'd been in a race that never stops, but when I married, and the challenge ended, all I had been running from kept moving forward and crashed on me in one giant abysmal heap.

Such a condition demands extreme measures. I had worn out Henry's patience, and for the sake of our marriage and family, it was time for him to take the bull by the horns.

Unlike Linda's husbands, Henry knew when to go to the wall. After three years of marriage and in the heat of an argument, he told me to "shape up or ship out," and he wasn't whistling Dixie; he meant business. Despite his even temper, Henry, no pushover, issued his ultimatum as a constructive wake-up call. But I was already aroused, at least to some degree.

I had heard the distant bugle call soon after an appointment Mother hastily made for Henry and Katie and me to have our picture taken by her former employer J.F. Knox who was soon to retire.

"This is your last chance to be photographed by him," Mother begged.

The photograph is disturbing, even to this day. Sour and impatient for no earthly reason, I had snapped at our sixteenth-month-old and caused her to cry shortly before the camera clicked. I put on my happy face, but Katie will forever have tears in her eyes. Those tears haunted me from the wall, especially after I learned I was pregnant with another child.

Mirrors don't lie, and mine reflected an ugly truth: I had a Cruella de Vil inhabiting me. *Oh, fearful pawn.* I opted to "shape up"—a change of husbands wouldn't change me. That, I knew, but I feared there was no hope for me.

My self gnawed at me even when Katie was but a tiny baby. The pediatrician gave all new mothers a suggested daily schedule. "Bathe at ten o'clock." Even if she was asleep, I woke her for bath time when the clock struck ten. Structure! Structure! It gets worse. While bathing this sweet child, I seldom smiled or interacted with her. Engaged but unengaged. Remember the shark incident when I lingered off to the side?

Unable to be the mother I had aimed for and the wife Henry warranted, I sought a psychiatrist's help for months. He suggested Henry and I go to church, and at the end of the session commented, "Joan, you sure would look good in a wet suit, like diver's wear." *A wet suit? Seriously?* I didn't buy a wet suit and never returned to him, but with no other recourse, we acted on his advice to attend church. However, the church I chose didn't believe in evil, suffering, or sickness. They believed evil, sickness, and death were illusions.

"Joan, don't ever mention that place again," Henry insisted.

"Don't worry, I won't. Those people don't live in the real world."

We never darkened their doorway again—I am a realist, unwilling to shelve my brain in exchange for help or relief.

Another dead end. To me, religion burdened people with lists of things to do and not do. Perform! Perform! That tried approach hadn't worked for me. Pulling myself up by my own bootstraps was easier said than done; I needed outside intervention.

Aware of my efforts by seeking counsel, Henry remained patient. Five months after his ultimatum, my friend Carol Whatley pleaded with me to meet her employer. I knew she was up to something as she ushered me into his plush office where he asked about my life. After a series of questions and hearing my complaints, he spoke of Jesus Christ—his life and death and how God, in Christ, was reconciling the world to himself.

I'd heard this foolishness before in college, and it caused the hair on my neck to bristle. *Is it just me, or is everybody allergic to this kind of talk?*

But when he assured me if I relied on Christ alone, God would change me from the inside out and give me joy and peace in the meantime, the stranger had my attention.

"You don't have to earn it. In fact, you can't. Any effort on your part to deserve the gift means you haven't sincerely embraced it. Take it! That, my dear, is when God takes over without condemnation. He's a loving father who forgives and forever accepts you and gives you a new heart with new desires, *if* you accept the work of his son on your behalf."

This stranger, in his luxurious office behind that fine mahogany desk was educated and the president of a successful business, and I believed the man.

God outmaneuvered my cynicism that day and led me on a path where life's major questions would be answered: *Where did I come from?* I was made by God. *Why am I here?* To find happiness in Christ by loving him and others. *Where am I going?* I'm going to be with him and, one day, live on a new earth with a physical body where everything this world has to offer is restored without the suffering.

Even before I returned home, the distress of bringing another child into my harsh, robotic world vanished; a joyful song displaced the dirge in my heart. My problems didn't go away, but I was changed. Something was different, and different was good.

Edna St. Vincent Millay expressed a similar experience in her poem, "Renascence":

> *Ah! Up then from the ground sprang I*
> *And hailed the earth with such a cry*
> *As is not heard save from a man*
> *Who has been dead, and lives again.*

I now had a foundation to move forward, and God began the lifelong process of overshadowing the Cruella de Vil in me. Two hours after meeting with Carol's boss, I skipped inside the house and announced excitedly, "Henry, I became a Christian today!"

"Oh, really? Well, you're the most unchristian Christian I've ever known," he said with a little smirk. I merited his assessment, but time would tell, I thought, unsure of what lay ahead. Henry, a good man, didn't perceive his own need. Sometimes our despicable goodness keeps us at bay from God.

I gave birth to Meg a month later and delighted in bath time. I kissed and caressed her, smiled and laughed, cooed and let her kick and splash to her heart's content. And I never woke her from sweet slumber. I cannot express how effortless and genuine that change was.

Henry's interest now piqued because of a difference in me— he entrusted himself to Christ the same month. Though still flawed people, we were safe, loved, and changing from the inside out.

Interestingly, the marriage grew worse before improving. Years prior, I had scrapped the notion of a *Father Knows Best* family and entered into wedlock with low standards. Now, my expectations soared into realms unrealistic—but at least I was emotionally engaged—heart and soul.

We attended and joined a church, but my thinking was faulty and required a six-month demolition on a massive scale. I had to come to terms with the fact that whereas our deepest longings may be noble and legitimate, they will never be fully satisfied in this life because we were designed for another world. That truth dismantled my unrealistic expectations in this thorny life and was a necessary first step in the process of building something of value.

*Henry and I at our
nephew's wedding
reception in 2016.*

*With Henry at Meg's
wedding reception in 1998
at Vestavia Country Club.*

10

SILVER LININGS

"**C**OME ON, EVERYBODY, LET'S GET GOING!" HENRY called from outside, after methodically loading the station wagon in June of 1976. I was twenty-nine. We now had three daughters and were on a spur-of-the-moment beach trip for five days with Mother, Susan, and her family. Hyped up, Katie, Meg, and Libby jumped in the car.

As I started out behind them, an inexplicable forewarning stopped me. Paralyzing, actually. The impression gripped with the same surety that the sun will rise tomorrow: "Look around—you will never see this again." Such concrete, voiceless revelations come maybe once in a lifetime, if at all.

Will we be in a car wreck? Whatever tomorrow held, I was seeing our home on Carla Circle for the last time. Of this, I was certain. For reasons unappreciated at the time, I rushed to the den and hastily wrote out two random Bible verses on a four-by-six index card and tucked the card in the frame of our bedroom mirror. Then I looked around for the last time before leaving and locking the door.

Rather than share with Henry what happened ("Joan, that's ridiculous!" he'd say), I pondered what just occurred. I was curious about why I'd been prompted to write out verses, especially those particular verses. Equally curious and uncharacteristic, Henry, always eager to get a move on, didn't blow the horn urging me to hurry up.

We arrived safely at the beach. Then Linda showed up unexpectedly with her three children in tow, which irritated Mother to no end. Even though Linda rented a motel room of her own just as Henry did, Mother preferred children in small doses, and the swirling bedlam and demands of more children upset her. We were glad Linda came because swirling fun followed Linda too.

Henry kept the brood entertained in a huge canvas blow-up boat Linda had purchased at no small price. Linda's extravagance also bothered Mama. "She breezes into a store flinging that purse behind her, and all the salespeople ignore me and rush to cater to her. She must be in high cotton because she spends money like she thinks she's the Queen Mother."

"I know. Let's just hope she has a coffer full of it," I said.

Henry was tickled when Mama nicknamed him Father Goose that trip because she admired his parenting. Mother's descriptions of people were spot-on but not always complimentary. In this case, she nailed Henry, a father deserving of her portrayal.

Night after night the two played Parcheesi whenever we went to the beach, and she relished Henry's attention and mutual love of puzzles and board games but teased him when he kept referring to the rules. "You're a stickler for the instructions all right, but they won't help you." Sure enough, she beat him eight times out of ten, but they enjoyed each other's jesting and wisecracks. And Henry never, ever, ever, *ever* gave up trying to outdo her.

"Your mother can be so much fun, but when it comes to Parcheesi, she shows no mercy!" my competitive husband noted with affection.

Our third night, Father Goose cooked grouper for everyone. At four o'clock in the morning, the phone rang. Daddy had received a call around midnight to say our house was on fire and had raced to the scene. Awake all night, Daddy told Henry the news and added, "Don't expect to be able to come back here and live."

Ever since the day we left, I had believed I was seeing our house for the last time, but the "you will never see this again" missive could have been far worse. I could have died in the gulf or in a car wreck. Or we all could have died.

But I was alive, shaking and crying, unable to produce a single tear. I dry-heaved. "We've lost everything, Henry! We've lost everything!"

"No, we haven't," he said, nodding toward our daughters, ages seven, five, and two. They snuggled together in the bed next to ours without a care in the world, exactly as we wanted. After several futile attempts to console me, Henry had the gall, the unmitigated nerve, to go back to sleep!

I was God's problem now and yearned for the peace Henry possessed, but it was impossible for one human to impart to another. I pleaded, "Lord, are you outside this destruction? How can I bear the loss of our possessions and family photographs?" Those were my two sole concerns, and my emotions raged against my theology as I wrestled with God.

My emotions shrieked, "You're being punished!"

My emotions warned, "You'll never get through this!"

My emotions sneered, "God isn't near!"

And finally, a "sweet sound" whispered, "This is your biggest test of faith yet, as a new believer."

Now on the verge of experiencing my theology, deeply and without pretense, I struggled honestly with God.

I was awake and feeling alone. Then the Romans verse written three days earlier gently came to mind: "O, the depth of the riches both of the wisdom and knowledge of God! How unsearchable are his judgments, and his ways past finding out" (Romans 11:33 KJV).

Thank you! I don't understand what you're doing, but I know you love me, and I trust you're in this mess. Mystery shrouded in calamity aside, I knew God was up to something good. But what about our possessions—the things I cherished? Then the second verse I wrote flooded my mind: "Your testimonies are my heritage forever, for they are the joy of my heart" (Psalms 119:111 ESV).

Nothing compared or competed with God's "testimonies," his word and promises. Rejoicing in those testimonies would change me and display the goodness he alone deserves. The rest was stuff, not an eternal "heritage"—such a rich word.

God used my pain, sleeplessness, and the verses that night to deal with my soul: my mind, will, and emotions. How kind of God in his foreknowledge to move on my behalf and prepare me for what lay ahead this night and in the months to follow. As I meditated on the verses in light of my questions, I joined Henry in restful sleep.

Daddy assumed we took to the road immediately and expected us home by ten o'clock that morning. He waited in a lawn chair in Mrs. Nelson's front yard where she and other neighbors hosted him until we arrived at three. Instead of disturbing the others before the crack of dawn, we waited to tell them at seven-thirty. We all packed up and left the beach at nine-thirty.

Everyday, Mrs. Nelson, an elderly Jewish widow, gave our dog cheddar cheese from Browdy's, the finest delicatessen in town. This day, she also gave Daddy a stiff bourbon and Coke.

We drove home not knowing what awaited, but as we turned onto Carla Circle, my eyes rested on friends and neighbors gathered around the circle, including our minister, Dr. Bill Hay.

Then I noticed the caved-in roof and partially charred outer shell of the house. *Oh, no.* Buddie's little angels were in the attic with other Christmas decorations. Gone forever.

"I found someone to board up all the windows," Daddy declared with pride, "so looters can't get in." Henry inspected our home, inside and out, while I visited with neighbors who

Our home after the fire.

told me "the flames were twice as tall as the house," lighting up the dark night. The house suffered major smoke and water damage, and the insurance company declared it a total loss.

"One of the fire truck's snorkels dug a hole six feet deep in our backyard and flung the melted, stretched kitchen phone high up in the pecan tree!" Henry chuckled as he reported back. "Oh, and by the way, all our family photos are safe and in good shape. Somehow, the combination of water and heat created a vacuum in the den cabinets and sealed the doors shut." And to think, the night before, I had wondered if God cared.

I chose not to go inside the house that day—I needed to go in alone the next day, a bittersweet moment. Such devastation! It looked and felt as if I'd been ravaged by some evil entity, but I knew God could take the ashes and acrid stench and make us better for it.

We'd been ravaged, all right. Shortly before Henry and the girls came behind me, I realized we'd also been burglarized. "Where's the silver chest with all our flatware?" I asked him. Gone. Collectors' plates were missing, as were two antique clocks. "Where're my engagement and wedding rings?" I had left them behind with costume jewelry still lying in place under the wet insulation on the scorched bedroom dresser.

When our friend Peggy Frese learned of my vanished rings, she came and sifted through the deep wet insulation on the dresser and floor searching for them.

"Joan, she must love ya'll a lot," Mama said. "Come here, you've got to see this. She's been digging so long her fingers are bleeding." The sight of Peggy's bloody hands made me cry, and although my rings were gone, our family photographs had been graciously spared.

The detective told us the thieves entered the bedroom window near the dresser, where I had placed the verses and my rings. "We're certain the fire started in the attic, but we don't know if they purposefully set it or if it was an accident from a match or cigarette."

*Stages of rebuilding
of our new home.*

If burglary and possible arson weren't already troublesome enough, we learned we were underinsured due to the rapid increase in house values in our neighborhood. We needed to salvage all we could. Neighbors collected dishes and silver to polish and store, and pillows, towels, and bedding to wash.

A week later, Dr. Hay and other men from our church undertook a major bulk of the demolition by hauling debris to a huge dumpster as big as a train car in our driveway. Henry and five church members with wheelbarrows sprinted back and forth as if in some sort of competition, but our minister paced himself at a slower, steady stride.

"I'm gonna go grab you guys some lunch," I said. "I'll be back in a bit." When I returned, six exhausted men were sprawled under the pecan tree while Dr. Hay continued pushing his wheelbarrow up and down the ramp at his constant pace—a tortoise-and-the-hare moment, to be sure.

"Let's dig out this Oriental rug and take it to the cleaners," Mama heard me comment to a gathering crowd of friends.

"Joan, there's no hope for this rug. It's burned black and will never look the same."

"But, Mama, Aunt Amy gave it to me. All I can do is try. Maybe they can cut off the burned edges and clean it several times."

"I think you've lost your mind."

Although I normally deferred to sober-mom, we hired a company to restore my fairy godmother's gift to me and used it for many years, although it never looked the same, just as Mama predicted.

My merciful sister Linda stored in her basement what furniture could be refinished or refurbished and opened her home to us. She settled Henry and me in the master bedroom and made sleeping arrangements for our children, along with her own three children, and pampered us for several days.

The word spread quickly. Each time the doorbell rang, which was often, Linda or I answered to receive items from friends and strangers: toys for the girls, pajamas, clothes, and food. But the items I'll never forget were from Judy Haise. She pampered me, too, when she appeared bearing a bottle of nice champagne and a beautiful new pink nightgown.

After leaving Linda's, we settled in a hotel suite for weeks before renting an apartment. The hotel's pool on those hot summer days was an oasis in the desert, providing fun and relief and a place for friends to visit us with their children.

We found a two-bedroom apartment in Homewood, but it needed furniture, which we also rented. For lack of space, Libby slept in a crib set up in the large master bedroom closet. As I looked around at the small dwelling with cheap, unattractive Danish modern furniture, I felt liberated. "Let's go to the pool!" All summer we pranced to the pool, only steps away from our door, while Henry dealt with the insurance company.

About the time I thought life might settle down, I met Carol Hurd, a former ballerina who also lived in the apartments. Carol taught me exercises we performed together, which resulted in two badly injured necks. Her thoughtful orthopedist admitted her to a hospital and placed her in traction for days, but my less-sympathetic orthopedist sent me home with a neck brace and traction-contraption to hang over a door. Carol had no children and could summon help at the push of a button, but here I was, with three little girls running around, hanging under a door.

Then September came. School started, and it was time to get down to brass tacks. We had a house to rebuild. Katie attended second grade at Crestline Elementary from eight until three; Meg attended kindergarten from nine until twelve; and Libby was on my hip each time we met with the builder.

My mischievous water-balloon-throwing childhood friend Glenda Trotter had married a home builder. Her husband Steve Swalley rebuilt our house at a compassionate price, and he and the designer found a way to stay within our budget and enlarge our home from a one-story, two-bedroom, two-bath house to one-and-a-half stories with four bedrooms and three baths.

It wasn't the ballerina's fault when October came, and I broke the "ballerina bone" in my foot by slipping sideways off a wedge shoe, although it was ironic. I dragged a hard cast ball-and-chain for six weeks as I drove around town transporting children to and from school and making important choices for the house. Miracle of miracles, I also carried joy (and Libby on my hip).

In November, we moved into the much larger house. Soon after Linda married her second husband in our new home, I answered the phone to hear an elderly lady's voice—a voice I'd never heard before. She didn't introduce herself but simply said, "Dearest, I'm calling to remind you that God's dealings with believers are never punitive, but always educatory."

"Oh, thank you so much." I already knew the truth she spoke, but something about her words and voice caused the reality to sink deeper than I thought possible.

Then, *click*. She ended the conversation.

Well, that was odd. Educatory? I'd never heard that word before in my life and haven't since, but it communicated and bathed me in a heavenly balm, especially after the ordeal of a house fire, burglary, injured neck, and broken foot, all within four months. I must have been God's needy student in need of a crash course.

A few months later, Daddy received an unexpected call too.

"Sax! Sax, I'm… I'm in jail!" Mama stammered. After an afternoon at Elizabeth's kitchen table in Mt. Brook—Birmingham's equivalent of Camelot—she veered her car off the road and plowed into a family's yard, making mincemeat of their mailbox. The police were called, took one look at her, drove her to the pokey, and escorted her to a cell.

As the alcohol wore off, Mama grew aware of her accommodations and complained to an officer about the uncomfortable bed and pillow.

"Mrs. Lawrence, must I remind you? You're in the Mt. Brook City Jail, not the Holiday Inn." Daddy bailed her out just as he did for Jadie Bell's son years ago.

When Mother and Daddy recounted this incident to my sisters and me, they laughed. So I laughed too. I suppose it was easier to laugh than to cry on top of everything else we'd been through, and, besides, very little shocked me about life with Mama.

11

CRUNCH TIME

———————

THE LAST TIME I SAW MY FATHER, I WAS THIRTY-SIX, AND I crawled onto his lap for the first time in many, many years.

For several months I had harbored a bad attitude toward Daddy because he made a point of not showing preferential treatment by paying Henry a little less than he paid other employees.

I could have intervened—Daddy would have done almost anything for me—but I didn't. Instead, I nursed a grudge. I also begrudged Linda because when she wanted something for herself or her children, she charged the purchases to Daddy, but I never did. No, I was a self-righteous prig, making the right choice but with a lousy rotten attitude.

The Sunday before Daddy died in 1984, the guest preacher assured us that nothing is allowed to touch our lives without a purpose and for our good. "Are you struggling with a problem beyond your control? Are you allowing it to steal your joy and peace? How's your heart? If you're angry with someone, you're only harming yourself and contaminating others. Guard your heart at all cost—it's the *only* thing you can control. I invite you to perform a mental exercise: take your problem, place it in a box, wrap it in beautiful paper, put a lovely bow on it, and read the card, 'To (insert your name), Love, God.'"

I did it. I put Henry's salary, Linda, and the unfairness in a box and accepted it from a perfect heavenly father. Embracing the gift, I plunged deeper into freedom—freedom from self pity and spite, and free to accept my earthly father's choice with inexplicable peace. And mercy, excessive mercy, the same mercy God had shown me.

Although Daddy knew nothing of my anger, I did, and I couldn't get to him fast enough. I hurried to the house that Sunday afternoon and curled up in his lap.

"Are you okay, Ponzie? Is something wrong?"

"No, Daddy, nothing's wrong. I just want to be close to you and tell you how much I love you."

"I love you too."

Two nights later, after a full day's work, our seventy-three-year-old father died of a massive heart attack at home. His water glass still had ice in it when I arrived after Susan's call. *How kind of God, in his foreknowledge to do a work in my heart and give me time with Daddy, time that was pure and real and sweet, instead of bitter regret.*

Now I understood why and how Jadie Bell overcame difficulty.

On a cool, sunny March afternoon, Daddy was buried, and the flag outside Homewood City Hall flew at half-staff. I have a picture of the flag, surrounded by a blossoming cherry tree. How poignant: one signaling death; the other bursting with life.

I'm fortunate to have Daddy's tobacco can, and the tobacco in it remains as he left it the night he died. "[T]hings have a terrible permanence when people die," penned Aline Kilmer in her poem, "Things." My sentiments exactly when I peer into Daddy's tobacco can.

Daddy's sudden death weighed heavily on Mother. Their life together had mellowed during the last few years. As Daddy became less short-fused, Mama responded by becoming more enjoyable, and the two-way street conveyed their relationship from barely tolerable to one of tender affection.

My devoted father at age sixty-four with his widow's peak, smoking his pipe, 1974.

Daddy's tobacco can, a few of his pipes, his gavel, and the photo of the flag at half-staff.

Several months after Daddy's death, Mama wasn't feeling well. "My heart is beating so fast I can barely catch my breath," she said when I phoned.

"I'll be right there."

I drove her to the doctor, and she entertained me with her charm while we waited in the exam room for the internist, whom I'll fittingly refer to as Dr. Dullard. He and a recently hired young physician entered to examine Mother.

For some reason that made no sense, Dr. Dullard looked at Mama and said, "Go home and pack what you need and report to Montclair Hospital. I think you're having a heart attack."

Taken aback, the younger doctor blurted, "She's not having a heart attack!"

"I'll handle this," Dr. Dullard shot back, unwilling to reconsider his opinion or concede to his colleague.

Confused and embarrassed for both men, we opted to err on the side of caution and drove home to gather Mother's belongings. She handled emergencies considerably better than day-to-day life and remained characteristically calm. However, on the way to the hospital, "I Want to Know What Love Is" played on the car radio. When Foreigner sang the soulful chorus, I noticed her chin quiver as she fought back tears. I revered sober-mom, who was modest and private, and held back my own tears.

Why didn't I just stop the damn car so we could both cry our hearts out together? It could have been a moment.

After we arrived at the hospital, a cardiologist confirmed the young whipper-snapper's opinion. Mama wasn't having a heart attack. Mama was broken-hearted.

*Daddy and Mother celebrating a happy
occasion at Great Aunt Amy's in 1969.*

12

FOR CRYING OUT LOUD

───────────────────

T WENTY YEARS AGO, LONG AFTER MY PARENTS' DEATHS, I sat in the ear, nose, and throat doctor's waiting room. I laid down the magazine and noticed a poor-looking mother and son—probably eight years old—enter. *Poor darlings.* As they sat across from me, I wondered what the boy's deprived life must be like. *It must be awful to be so poor... I hope he has a dad... gee, they look pitiful.*

"Mom," he asked, "am I going back to school after this?"

"We'll see, sweetie. It depends on how long we're here. Do you wanna go back to school?"

"Yep."

"You wanna read one of your schoolbooks together while we wait?"

"Yeah, my reading book!" After he retrieved the book, she nestled him under her wing, and they took turns reading. She asked questions about the story and they laughed. While they interacted so sweetly, I sobbed like a sniveling baby right there in the waiting room because they were making a memory I didn't have.

What a fortunate little boy!

If only I had resembled an indigent person or a cur dog, Mama might have taken me under her wing. Then again, there must have been something currish about me since Mama said my recessed chin reminded her of Andy Gump, a completely chinless, strange-looking comic-strip character. I began jutting out my jaw to compensate for my obvious lack of a chin.

Wise-cracking Mother had a flair for chipping away at our self-identity and worth.

My few memories of her touch centered on my nose. She pinched and massaged it in such a way that I knew her intention was to remodel my nose and bring it to a point. "What a cute pug nose you have," others said. But Mama didn't think so.

At the age of forty-one, after Mother died, I saw a plastic surgeon. The nurse entered the patient room first, looked at me, and asked, "Are you here for a rhinoplasty?"

"Nope, I'm keeping this nose. Just give me a chin." I wanted to look better, not different, and I wear my nose as a badge of honor.

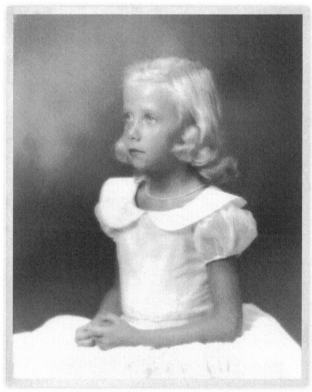

A photo taken right after Mama pinched my nose.

13

INSIDE THE BLACK HOLE

===

L INDA RACED TO MY HOUSE LATE ONE MORNING WHEN
I was thirty-five and bounded from her car after having
been at Mother's. In the throes of washing dishes, I looked from
the kitchen window and noticed her resolute gait and furrowed
brow. This was no ordinary visit.

Bursting through the door, Linda bellowed, "Joan, Joan! I
know why Mama drinks! Everything makes sense now." She flung
her purse on the living room sofa and rubbed her temples. "Oh,
God, our whole life makes sense!" Trying to calm her and brace
myself for a first view into the black hole, I sat to hear the story.

"I just left Mama's. I was in her bathroom having abdominal
cramps. The pain was awful, and I cried and screamed. Then
Mama came to the bathroom door.

"Stop it! Stop it right now!' she yelled at me.

"I can't help it, Mama.'"

Screaming and crying for what surely seemed like a lifetime
to both of them, Linda's bathroom experience unearthed memories and images no longer possible for Mama to hide. Given
a little time, she might have collected herself and escaped this
reckoning day, but suppressed flashbacks from the past were
jerked into the present with no time for composure.

"I walked back to the den," Linda continued. "Mama was in her lounge chair, curled in the fetal position, and sober in every way. I've never seen her so reflective or heard her so monotone.

"Mama? Are you okay?"

"Sit down," she told Linda. "I have something to tell you. Eighteen months after Joan was born, I was on the same toilet crying just like you," she recounted with a fixed and faraway look in her glazed eyes.

"Daddy and Doug were trying to get their business up and running, and I was pregnant. We were afraid we couldn't afford another child, so friends persuaded us to have an abortion. I was taken somewhere, I don't remember where, but afterward, the doctor said I would abort at home.

"Then he stared me down with a stern warning, 'Look at me! I don't ever want to see you again.'"

"Don't worry, you won't," Mama replied.

Jadie Bell, our ever-present buffer, sat on the edge of the bathtub by Mama's side until she lost the unwanted child, a little boy. Linda didn't ask how far along she was in the pregnancy, but when Jadie Bell and Mama were startled to see the boy—no doubt, it was a boy—regret and sorrow overtook Mama. Regret and sorrow (those pitiless twins) swept Mama up in their fierce grim claws.

"It was a little person, Linda, not something to flush away."

The empty can will suffice as a tiny coffin, thought Jadie Bell. Soda crackers came in tin cans at the time. Cradling the tin box, she ventured up the hill behind our home, dug a hole, and pushed the can deep into the ground, burying our brother and any chance of passing on our father's name. Jadie Bell Thomas carried our parents' secret to her own grave.

"At two o'clock in the morning," Mama forged ahead still in a fetal position, "I ran to the woods and like a woman gone mad, I dug the ground, clawing the earth. I want my baby, I want my son! What have I done, Linda? I'll never forgive myself. Don't tell anyone. You can't ever tell. Promise me you won't tell."

Linda assured our tormented mother of forgiveness. "I forgive you, Mama, I do. And you can know God's forgiveness if you'll accept it, but I have to tell Susan and Joan. They deserve to know. This explains everything. You can't let them go on without answers. I'm so glad you told me, and I know they'll forgive you." Oddly, Mother didn't protest.

At my kitchen table, Linda and I cried, and my mind reeled with questions: "Where exactly is he buried, Linda? Did Mother and Daddy make the decision together, or were they at odds with one another?"

"I wish I knew, Joan. I didn't ask for details. You had to be there to appreciate why I didn't press in."

I hurried to Mama, cradled her under my wing, and rocked her. We rocked and cried and spoke few words. All she needed, I thought, was to be fully known, accepted, and forgiven. From the depths of my heart, I forgave her, and the subject was never broached again. Ever. I regret not having answers to my questions, but Linda was right. You had to be there.

Linda, Susan, and I met soon afterward. We were suffering too, but in need of many words as we began putting puzzle pieces in place, trying to understand the revelation's impact on our history and its ongoing personal ramifications too complex to understand or describe.

We now understood their lamentable choice was why Mama drank and why our parents argued. It's why Daddy spoiled her and thought he was protecting us with two maids. It explained Mother's moaning self-hate to the mirror. It's why I felt neglected. It's why she was never happy for us when we were pregnant. It's why Daddy chose distraction over remedy, and in the wake of it all was a hovering, bitter sadness that engulfed our home and souls.

As my sisters and I talked, the Gordian knot was attacked from every angle, and each feeble attempt at unraveling helped explain everyone's behavior, every remembered incident, every action and reaction all these many years. Her alcoholism resulting from the abortion set into motion years of damage to her marriage, and the harm to us girls was palpable and more difficult to forgive.

"I remember them as happy and in love until I was seven," Linda said again. "That must have been after the abortion, when Mama started drinking. She sure made life miserable, didn't she?"

"Yes, she did," I answered. "I was so full of anger and dread, I... I can't even explain it."

"You know it's why I eloped so young."

Yes, I did.

"Susan, how did you manage to seem so tranquil most of the time? You never threw away her alcohol, and you didn't talk to her the way Linda and I did," I asked.

"Oh, yes I did! And if I *seemed* tranquil, it's only because I learned to suppress and ignore my feelings."

Linda sighed. "Well, it definitely caused the three of us to be closer than we would've been otherwise."

"That's for sure," Susan and I said in unison.

"But she screwed up my life big time!" Linda declared.

Yes, but no. We each made our own choices, but Linda was right on one level—there was no refuting or denying that we were still those same little girls in grown-up bodies. Our childhood didn't go away just because some years had passed.

"We had a brother. Oh, God, we *have* a brother," we said as one voice.

The sorrow that overtook our mother had taken her away from us. *Oh, the sadness we carry for what might have been. If only Mama and Daddy had walked into that dark place together and sought help.* Life is replete with "if only... it could have been so good."

We never told Daddy about Mother's confession. Maybe we should have—I don't know. We didn't decide not to tell; it wasn't even discussed. We were three wounded buddies with an unspoken understanding that hurting him at this point would serve no constructive purpose. Too many years had elapsed.

Daddy, we thought, had his own regrets, and we shielded him from any pain within our control. What more can I say? It was our way of life.

Besides, all that mattered was that he was safe. In his late forties, Daddy attended courses at a Bible college and studied evidence for Christ's resurrection. "Once convinced of that," he assured me as we sat on their back porch when I was twenty-eight, "I had no choice but to believe and rely on all of his claims." A broken man—as we all are—but safe. Mother was broken, too, but not safe. Not safe at all.

14

FROM EATING ROCK TO STANDING ON ONE

========================

MOTHER HAD DISPLAYED A BIZARRE HABIT WHEN WE were children. "There she goes again!" we all giggled to one another when Mama walked outside, chiseled a piece of the soft rock wall and ate it. This happened with regularity. However, ingesting rock didn't satisfy her strange craving.

One year after Mother's death in 1987, I scheduled an appointment for our sixteen-year-old daughter Meg to see the pediatrician because of a lump on her neck (which turned out to be nothing), but when the doctor noticed how pale she appeared, he drew blood for analysis. A few minutes later he streamed back in. "This number can't be right. I need to take more blood and redo the test."

After the second round, he returned with a serious tone. "She's so anemic, I don't know how she had the strength to walk in here. We need to get her to a hematologist right away. In the meantime, she needs iron." I panicked and served her rare steak for dinner, buying time until the appointment with the hematologist a few days later.

Meg was diagnosed with von Willebrand disease, a primarily hereditary disorder. Those with von Willebrand lack

My pale mother in her fifties.

a blood clotting factor, and though not as serious as hemophilia, females lose abnormal amounts of blood during their menstrual periods and become severely anemic without additional iron.

Typically, anemics crave dirt or ice. Mama ate rock; Meg crunched ice. Mama frequently said she felt her best during pregnancy. No wonder! Otherwise, she lost massive amounts of blood every month. She was fatigued, pale, and somewhat cloistered much of her life. When Mama pled, "Lord, give me strength!" I thought she was being dramatic, but Mama's petition was sincere.

Her inadequate physician, Dr. Dullard, knew for years she was unacceptably anemic, but rather than refer her to a hematologist or simply peruse his medical books on the subject, he continued to administer useless B12 shots. Why didn't he know better? All she needed were iron supplements and other precautionary measures. But who knew? Certainly not Dr. Dullard.

I look back at photographs and see Mother so ghostly white. Her fledging red blood cells never had a chance to mature and nurture her.

This same doctor withheld from Mother for an entire year the diagnosis of lung cancer when she was only sixty-five. "Why in the world didn't you tell us?" I grilled him on the phone in January of 1987.

"I didn't want to upset her," the doc with the God-complex asserted. I wanted to give him some sailor talk, and I knew the words. I learned them from a Merchant Marine, my father.

To his credit, Dr. Dullard had attempted to persuade Mama to quit smoking. He even showed her framed slices of two lungs: a healthy pink nonsmoker's lung and a blackish Swiss cheese-looking slice of a smoker's lung.

"See there," he said with the upper hand. "Now, what do you have to say?"

"Well, they're both dead, aren't they?"

"You're just too much." He laughed. "I give up on you. I've said all I can say."

But when Mother's lung had cancer, she wanted to live and immediately quit her fifty-year smoking habit. At last under the care of an oncologist, she received radiation therapy, but the treatment came at least a year too late. (Linda said we probably should have "sued the quack" for the sake of his other patients and those who came after us.)

After the diagnosis, Linda and I went to see Mama. I sat in a chair, while Linda sat at her feet and spoke of Christ as our only hope to one day be on a new earth with new bodies where everything is restored, with art, music, literature, recreation, work, travel, and all this world has to offer without the sadness.

I had spoken of this high-stakes matter with Mama in the past to no avail.

This day, however, Linda's words hit a chord, and God drew Mama to himself. Having forgiveness from Linda, Susan, and me was nice, but God's acceptance, compassion, and companionship in Christ was life-changing. She awoke the next morning excited and at peace, bubbling over with joy. I do not exaggerate. From January until November, she attended church with my family and blossomed as Mary Poppins (most of the time), and her drinking decreased considerably, but not altogether.

She still teased about my hair a few times. "Joan, every time you even start to look better, you go and get that hair cut!"

"You may be right, Mama, but with three teenage girls, I don't have time for a Rapunzel-do. It's all I can do to get both legs shaved on the same day." She liked my quick comeback and laughed.

In June, Mother had her last hoorah in Cape Cod with my family and Susan and her children (thanks to Aunt Amy's son, who offered his home on the Cape for a week). For months, Linda had agreed and planned to join us. She worked for the state of Virginia at a truck weigh-station at the time and was taking a week's vacation. On the day of our arrival in Cape Cod, Susan answered Linda's phone call.

"I can't come," she said. "I'm sorry, but a trucker beat me up, and I'm in the hospital."

"Linda, no! That's terrible! Are you all right?" Susan asked.

"I'll be okay. My face is just clobbered. Will you explain to Mama why I can't come?"

Worried how the news would affect Mother and our entire trip, Susan didn't let the matter drop and continued to push for more answers. At some point during the probing, when Linda hedged and couldn't explain crucial details, she realized Linda wasn't being forthcoming.

"This doesn't add up, Linda. Tell me the truth."

"All right, all right! I've just had a facelift, but don't tell Mama."

"Oh, so you'd rather her think a trucker assaulted you? No, Linda, I'm telling her and Joan the truth, and I'll never understand why you conjured up such a terrible story."

The *why* is mind-boggling, but two things were clear: Linda's excuse would have garnered attention and sympathy, and she was willing to miss our last hoorah with Mama.

Agreeable and sweet, Mama was a sport as we roamed Hyannis Port, Nantucket, and went whale watching in Providence.

"Whale at two o'clock," a man announced over the speaker. Mother stayed seated while the rest of us ran to the two o'clock position, sighting nothing. "Whale at ten o'clock." We all ran again but Mama didn't. After the boat docked, she quipped, "Ya'll should've just stayed in your seats 'cause I saw more whales than you did!"

Shortly before hospice was called in early that December, Mama and I had our last phone conversation. I had snapped at her about who knows what and called her back. "Oh, Mama, I'm so sorry for the way I just talked to you."

"That's okay, baby, I know your heart." We had many pleasant conversations after that, but those were her final words to me over a telephone.

On her deathbed later that month, Mama struggled to whisper, "Joan, I want to tell you something."

Expecting to hear something profound, I leaned in. "Yes, Mama, what is it?"

Witty to the end, she spoke, "Remember this about doctors. They're only practicing."

A vodka martini was still in the freezer when Mama died three weeks later. However her one-year-old Bible looked to be twenty years old—underlined, dog-eared, and tattered. Mama was on the right trajectory, and she knew where she was going.

15

CAN'T GET NO SATISFACTION

L INDA COULDN'T RELEASE MAMA'S GRIP ON HER, EVEN after Mother's confession. As the years passed, she went to a lonely place and hungered for contentment that circumstances and people cannot provide. Like a cat, she'd always landed on her feet, but her daughter Kim would soon liken her to "a horse running into a burning barn, taking others along with her."

After Earnest's death, Kim arranged for Linda's move to an assisted-living facility close to her own home. Fortunately, Earnest had pension and although he was up a financial creek with no paddle, he had continued making payments on his life insurance policy. If Linda managed her money, she wouldn't need to touch the principal.

"Linda, we know this isn't easy for you," Susan and I commented once she settled in, "but this is a nice place and so convenient to Kim."

"You think so? There's not enough closet space. I don't know why someone in the family doesn't take me in. That's what families are supposed to do." We changed the subject. Yes, she welcomed my family after our house fire. Susan, Kim, and I also received her into our homes for five months and learned there was no way to please the sister we once enjoyed and to whom we'd been so close. Hard as we tried, we couldn't meet Linda's expectations.

"The food is terrible," she said on our next visit, "and I think the people here are stealing from me. They barge in at night without any warning."

She refused to join others in the parlor, stroll the hall, or go to the dining room, and she paid personnel to bring her meals. After purchasing a new Lexus, Linda tuned back in to QVC and HSN and began shopping again. Kim paid the bills from Linda's money, organized her medicines by the week, and solved nagging problems that grew by the day.

So discontent was Linda that Kim agreed to move her again after three months—an exhaustive, time-consuming task. Kim and her boyfriend relocated her to an independent living facility with two bedrooms, two baths, and lots of closet space.

The home hosted cocktail hour with a piano player in the common area where many gathered and sang to songs of the 1930s, '40s, and '50s. A hair salon, library, weekly speakers, exercise classes, church on Sunday, a communal porch with tables and chairs, and an attractive dining room and restaurant were there for the taking. But Linda took no part. It seemed as though she was trying to punish someone.

Her lifestyle and worsening COPD necessitated that she be hooked up to oxygen at night. Linda purchased a scooter to go for meals, but because "no one" spoke to her, and she didn't like those who did, she quit after two weeks and paid extra to have meals delivered. She used the scooter only to meet us when we drove her to doctor appointments or coaxed her to go to lunch or TJMaxx.

Her Lexus became an issue on the first day. She phoned the director and told her to come upstairs "right this minute!" Susan, Kim, and I listened as Linda demanded a special parking place close to the front door.

"I'm sorry, Mrs. Browning, but we don't reserve parking places for residents. If you have a handicap sticker, you can park close to the building when a space becomes available."

When Linda became hostile and rude, I followed Dr. Krug's advice. I held her hand, looked her squarely in the eye, and calmly said, "Linda, I love you. I'm not walking away from you, but I am walking away from this." And I did.

Kim obtained a handicap sticker for her, but once Linda found the ideal parking spot, she never used the car again for fear of losing the prime location. "That Lexus is nothing more than an expensive paperweight," Kim sighed.

Thirteen months later, Linda received an invitation from an old boyfriend to spend a week with him in West Palm Beach, Florida. She sprang out of that bed lickety-split and onto a plane and had a marvelous time. But after returning home, she developed a severe lung infection and was admitted to a hospital.

No sooner than she was released, she developed sepsis and entered another hospital and then another after that. "We've done all we can for her. The infection and sepsis are cured, but her COPD won't improve," the pulmonologist told Susan and me. "It's only a matter of time. You need to understand she's no longer sustainable on her own."

Kim was advised to call in hospice. "Don't be alarmed. We have people who've been on hospice for over five years," they said to console us.

Kim moved Linda into a garden home close to her own and hired round-the-clock sitters, but Kim now realized she could never make her mom happy. "One of the sitters is trying to poison me," Linda said. It seemed once they heard all of Linda's riveting stories, she had no further use for them. She went through many sitters and lots of money, diving into the principal.

Solving Linda's issues with hospice and sitters—plus managing her mother's money, pills, and bills—exhausted Kim, and the tension between Kim and her boyfriend escalated. They went with Susan and me to Dr. Krug for counseling, but Kim didn't return for the next appointment, although the boyfriend did. "I'm sorry," Dr. Krug told him, "but if Kim refuses to come, I don't see how I can help you."

"I need something to cuddle with," Linda mentioned in a phone conversation. I assumed it was idle chatter, but when Kim left town for a weekend trip to a nearby lake, Linda used the opportunity to purchase a $4,000 Yorkie to cure the loneliness, heaping more guilt on Kim.

Then she thought the dog might be lonely too. Her solution? Buy yet another dog. When Kim dared to leave town again, Linda bought a Shih Tzu, but the aggressive Yorkie— that refused to be cuddled—constantly bit the Shih Tzu's eyes, and they had to be separated. While one dog roamed the house messing up the carpet, the other was placed in a child's playpen. Neither dog was allowed to enjoy the outdoors.

"A hawk will get them if I let them out," Linda said.

"Won't you let me take them outside if I hold them close to the leash?" I begged.

"No, a hawk'll get 'em."

Every attempt to reason with Linda on any subject was like trying to find one's way out of a house of mirrors.

Linda's last sitters, Patrice and Wondolyn, weren't hired to care for two dogs, but they did. (Nor were they hired to fill in paperwork and haul QVC and HSN packages to the UPS store, but they did.) Several months later, when the comfort and companionship Linda longed for eluded her, she gave the expensive dogs away.

Kim, now in a web from which she couldn't escape, made an appointment with Dr. Krug in the summer of 2017. At last ready to hear and heed his counsel, she received the advice too late. Linda was near death.

Kim phoned me the morning of July 10, 2017. "Hospice just told me Mom's in the beginning stage of dying." Susan, Aimee, and I raced over but by then Linda couldn't talk. The hospice nurse and both sitters attended to her as we, along with several of Linda's grandchildren and nieces, wandered in and out of the bedroom.

Late that evening, we said our goodbyes to Linda and spent the night. The next morning, while others waited in the living room or outside on the deck, Wondolyn and I had the singular privilege of holding Linda's hands when she left this world—with a perfect manicure and pedicure, thanks to Patrice. My restless, gypsy sister went to her true home to finally flourish in every way.

Earnest's ashes, along with those of her favorite dogs, were buried in the casket with Linda next to Daddy, as instructed.

After her mom's death, Kim cleared the house of valuables and hired a company to conduct an estate sale. Throughout the years, Linda moved no less than fourteen times, and I wondered how many family photographs, letters, and other sentimental items were overlooked in all the boxes stored in her garage.

"Kim," I asked, "may I come by the day before the sale and make sure nothing went unnoticed? And I'd like to purchase something of your mom's that's meaningful to me."

"Yes, of course. I'll arrange a time for you while the seller's here working."

As I walked into Linda's garage, lo and behold, I discovered—in a box piled high with worn-out or broken Christmas decorations—three of the original angels my grandmother Buddie had decorated at our kitchen table fifty-seven years earlier. And I had thought they were gone forever! So I ransomed her creations, scooped them up, and brought them home.

When my parents died, I was heartbroken and felt so very old; I was nobody's little girl anymore. When Linda died, I missed my long-lost soul mate, a tender branch that wouldn't bend, but because of God's unmerited grace, they had each been ransomed, scooped up, and brought home.

Buddie's recovered angels. God must have saved these throughout the years, because they survived Linda's many moves.

Linda, Susan, and me (left to right) at the beach three years before Linda's death.

16

USING THE PAST

M Y CHILDHOOD EXPERIENCES AND DISAPPOINTMENTS would not go wasted—neither would the nights I cried myself to sleep. As it turns out, nothing is intended to be wasted. I learned this lesson anew from John Glasser.

I first met seventy-nine-year-old John Glasser in 1995 when I was forty-eight. A retired attorney, he was a pillar in the community. "A visionary," people said of him. "A truly great man." He phoned one day and asked to meet me at the Homewood Library, and I jumped at the chance.

Two years earlier, burdened for under-resourced children who either couldn't read or were reading below grade level, he methodically established a nonprofit organization and named it Better Basics, Inc.

As executive director and sole fundraiser, he hired a devoted staff. Accepting the constant and heavy mantle, he recruited and paid retired teachers to help struggling readers and rallied volunteers to assist individual children with fluency, without which comprehension is virtually impossible. Principals welcomed his services.

When we met, Mr. Glasser asked me to serve on his board because of my involvement with the Alabama Reading

Initiative (ARI). As education chairman of Eagle Forum of Alabama, I had built rapport with the Alabama State Superintendent, who asked me to be one of five members of the ARI steering committee. For thirteen months, before launching the successful statewide initiative several years later, we studied the published, peer-reviewed, and replicated scientific research on reading.

"Will you join us, Joan?"

"Yes, Mr. Glasser, a thousand times, yes." In addition to serving on his board, I also volunteered to assist children with fluency, and with few heart-wrenching exceptions, I stayed on task.

Three years later, Better Basics received accolades from many sources, including the Alabama State Department of Education. Starting with one inner-city school in 1993, the program is now in forty-two schools throughout central Alabama.

In the midst of continuing with Better Basics, Mr. Glasser discovered that many of the students served didn't attend church and might never hear what he called "the best news in the world."

"Joan, I want to establish an after-school program to reach these little ones while their hearts are still tender," he said, and I saw his wheels spinning. "Grown-ups have a hard time accepting gifts and promises, but not little children. Will you help me get another program up and running and serve on its board?"

"Yes, Mr. Glasser, you know I will." Who could say no to this noble lionhearted giant of a gentleman who insisted on carrying my briefcase when he could barely carry his own? Moreover, I heard a "sweet sound" calling my name.

In 2003, eighty-seven-year-old John Glasser, a secretary, and I birthed another nonprofit organization with more funds to be raised, more volunteers to be recruited and trained, background checks to be conducted, a curriculum to be written, children to be invited, staff to be hired, and school supervisors to be placed onsite. He incorporated and named it Discovery Clubs.

Little did I know at the time that Discovery Clubs would afford me numerous opportunities to console many children who had heartaches incredibly similar to mine as a child.

The operation energized Mr. Glasser. "Top of the morning!" he boomed coming into board meetings and "Talley ho!" as he left or at the end of a phone conversation.

Having already developed warm relationships with the elementary school principals through Better Basics, they welcomed Mr. Glasser's after-school Bible clubs. One year later, we had more requests from principals than we could accommodate. We needed volunteers, lots of volunteers, in order to satisfy the flood of invitations we received.

Discovery Clubs still thrives and offers volunteers freedom to get to know the students—their cares, worries, hopes, joys. Its purpose is to be a fun hour once a week: games, songs, snacks, prizes, scripture memorization, and Bible stories about a real prince who leaves his father's house to rescue his lost treasure.

Some students come from intact families, but only a sad few live with a mother and father. One principal bemoaned that only twelve percent of her entire student population lived with two parents.

The majority of children walk home or go to after-school care at the end of club hour, and the remaining are picked up by car. When youngsters' rides didn't arrive at four o'clock, I understood their anxiety as they paced, looking up and down the road waiting for a parent or relative—anybody— to remember them. Forgotten or neglected children got my juices flowing, and I knew my crossing paths with them wasn't coincidental.

An unruly fourth grader by the name of Montrel almost caused me to pull my hair out and give up during my first year of volunteering. His behavior grew increasingly disruptive and frustrating. Finally, after all our disciplinary tricks failed, I walked him into the hallway while other volunteers continued conducting the class. We could have whisked the little hellraiser to the principal's office, but, first, I wanted a chance to talk with him alone.

"What's the matter, Montrel? Don't you like Discovery Clubs?" I asked as we sat on the floor.

He looked at his feet and whispered, "I don't like the Bible stories." It was the first time I ever heard that loud mouth whisper.

"That's okay," I said, "but the stories we tell you are true. The Bible isn't so much about you, Montrel. It's more about God and what he's done for you and what he wants to do for you. Maybe if you listen to the stories, you'll learn how much he loves you. Then you'll want to listen. Okay?"

"Okay."

"Anything else you wanna tell me?"

"No."

"All right, let's go back in."

I noticed the hands-on principal nearby watching us, and she caught my attention right before I followed in behind Montrel. As we met in the middle of the corridor, she quizzed, "You know about Montrel, don't you?"

"No, what's going on?"

"His father's in jail, and today his mother left for three months of drug rehab. It's sad." Indeed, it was, and my perspective of Montrel changed that day. This wide-eyed, wild kid was suffering unimaginable sadness at home, and he couldn't leave his misery at the school door. But I was no foreigner to heartache and understood why suffering kids often lash out or shut down. Convinced Montrel wasn't the only child facing trauma, my perception of all the children changed that day.

"You're safe here at Discovery Clubs," I promised them. "For this hour, you are safe. We love you no matter what, and we won't allow anyone to hurt you, but we won't permit you to hurt or be mean to anybody either. And we will never lie to you."

Weeks later, Montrel accidentally broke his glasses, but his family couldn't afford another pair. Volunteer Olivia Riddle had a son who worked at an optical store, and she suggested we take Montrel for an exam and new glasses. The owner was willing to absorb the cost, but first, we needed his grandmother's permission. Permission granted.

Olivia and I drove the fun-loving, well-behaved boy to the eye clinic. "Do you want to go to Chick-fil-A or McDonald's?" we asked afterward. He'd never heard of Chick-fil-A, so he chose the less expensive but familiar McDonald's. A week later, Montrel was presented with a pair of new glasses and, as an extra bonus, a pair of prescription sunglasses. He clasped them with excitement and gratitude.

It's been said when someone loves and trusts you, he's more likely to love your God. All I know is several weeks later Montrel went out of his way to tell us that he trusted Christ. All I can attest to is this live-wire became more attentive, more helpful, and better behaved. His classroom teacher reported the same. "A sight to behold!" she said, beaming. At last, he memorized scripture verses, but several months after our hallway conversation, Montrel never returned.

Oh, how I missed the little boy I almost gave up on. I'm consoled by the fact that the last verse he recited was Hebrews 13:5, which reads, "[God] will never leave you nor forsake you," and we defined "forsake" as "when someone turns and leaves you just when you need him the most."

Montrel was in God's hands now. Only his new friend and shepherd could be with him twenty-four-seven.

Similar stories were reported in other schools in our inner-city clubs and continue to this day. Many of the children's stories are shocking. An unacceptable number of these children are, without question, prematurely exposed to grown-up problems, as I was.

One child watched his uncle murdered in the alley behind his house; others witnessed their mom being beaten by a boyfriend; many had a parent in jail; and others lived with addicts. Most people go through life never having been confronted with what little ones are enduring.

My past had conditioned me to be shock-proof, and they must have known it. Children told me their stories and I told them mine—stories only my husband and sisters know—in our small group time or one-on-one in the hallway, depending on the appropriateness. When children begged, "Please take me home with you," I couldn't, but I could promise them God would go home with them, if invited.

That was no lie. No crutch. It was a life-changing promise that had stood the test of time.

"Sometimes I cry myself to sleep," children confided in me.

"Me too! Me too!" Then I told them why I wished I had known Christ as a kid. Was that a spark of hope I saw in those dark little eyes?

Once, while teaching fourth-grade girls, I showed them a large front-page newspaper picture of Condoleezza Rice. "Do you know where she grew up and went to school?" I asked.

"No."

"Right here in Birmingham. Maybe even close to you. Now look! She's the Secretary of State of all the United States. She was a young girl at one time just like you, but she studied hard, plowed ahead, and overcame difficulties." Was that a glimmer of aspiration I saw in some eyes?

"Close your eyes and open your hand," a shy third-grade boy implored at the end of club one day. I closed my eyes as he placed an object in my hand. Then he curled my fingers into a fist before dashing out the door. When I looked down, there in the palm of my hand was a braided bracelet he made for me. For me! I wore that bracelet the rest of the year—the gift was his and my little secret.

A note and drawing to me from Patrice, a third grade Discovery Club student in 2014.

Discovery Clubs is now in thirty schools with four hundred volunteers teaching two thousand children every week. It not only brings boys and girls the best news in the world, but also brings them hope, the kind of assurance Hebrews 6:19 says is "an anchor of the soul, both sure and steadfast" (NKJV).

Other unexpected, positive outcomes took place in the schools participating. Racial reconciliation occurred. One year, a second grader recoiled each time I reached out to her. The third time I extended my hands, she pulled back and said, "You're gonna hit me!"

"I would never, ever hit you."

"My mama told me not to talk to white people." I wondered what Rosie's mother had heard or what she had undergone at the hands of white people.

Amazingly, by the end of that very day, Rosie called me Mama. Our class met in the auditorium that year, and I braced myself against the stage because each time she entered, she ran the length of the auditorium at full-throttle and jumped into my arms. She wrapped around me like a koala bear and called me Mama the rest of the year.

A few weeks after clubs began, I noticed a woman sitting in the back corner. "That's my mama," Rosie said. I hurried to introduce myself and serve her the same snack we gave the girls. The mother was curious and seemed skeptical but stayed the entire hour. She must have approved of us and our teaching because she never visited again but continued to allow her daughter to come. We anticipated seeing Rosie the next year as a third grader, but like Montrel, she never returned.

Sometimes building rapport was with people of my own skin color. A white teacher at one of the schools disdained us. She was suspicious, rude, and accusatory, despite the fact that principals reported improved behavior and grades among Discovery Club children.

"Who do you think you are coming over the mountain to our school? Bunch of do-gooders!"

She stationed herself in the hall after school where we had to pass by and hurled nasty remarks at us. She intimidated and made some volunteers cry. This went on for several years. We were friendly and smiled, but it did no good. Then I watched a volunteer disarm her.

One day before the bell rang, volunteer Lex Williamson invested in her too by asking relevant questions regarding her life and work, and he listened attentively as if the rest of us were invisible. They were having a two-way conversation. It was magic. He wasn't patronizing, mind you, he simply showed interest in her, while the other nineteen of us chose to avoid her at all cost.

She actually mellowed a bit; her times in our path became fewer and fewer. I read a greeting card in 1972 that said, "Those who are the most difficult to love need love the most." Of course, we have no control over who accepts or rejects it.

My friendship with John Glasser enlarged my heart, and I am a better person because of the association. Now deceased, he set the stage for me to reach and encourage children who might otherwise be without the anchor. As I said, nothing is intended to be wasted.

The front steps of the Saulter Road house today and the window where I watched for Daddy to arrive home after work.

Mama and Daddy in 1943 with baby Linda on our front steps.

17

ENDING IN A WORLD
OF HURT

WHEN I GO TO SUSAN'S HOUSE, THE HOME OF OUR youth, I still drift to childhood memories, except the two distinct paths created by us girls and the Wellington Road children are now overgrown with weeds and bushes. The front porch and steps haven't changed since the house was built, and the brick and rock walls and garden steps remain, but the wretched kitchen table and booths are gone. All the doors and doorknobs are the same. Very little has changed; it just seems much smaller now, and I no longer focus on my bedroom window.

I'm sad when I scan the back property, wondering where our brother is buried, or when I note where Mama lay on the dining and living room floors. But I'm not angry anymore.

I wrote earlier that life is hard, and it is. When troubles come, I learn endurance. Waiting patiently but expectantly for resolution is beneficial for my mind, health, and relationships. Then, like a chain reaction, the patience leads to experience, and the experience brings hope, an assurance that doesn't delude or disappoint, and the process results in praise.

Years ago, Mary Glynn Peeples reminded our Bible class of a hard truth. "The circumstance of life, the events of life, and the people around me in life do not *make* me the way I am but *reveal* the way I am." This annoying fact constantly reveals the Cruella in me and requires that I own and adjust my own attitude and behavior—the only issues within my control.

"Be careful but take heart!" she encouraged us. "Don't beat yourself up over your first reaction. Pay attention to your second response. The time between your first and second response is dangerous ground. Pay close attention to what goes on inside of you when things happen outside of you because you *are* who you've been becoming."

I *am* who I've been becoming. I'd observed this bad news/ good news truth in Linda's life—and in my own. My first twenty-four years of accumulated unloving, angry reactions were turning me into a miserable, difficult, lonely creature, while accumulated kind responses are transforming me into a happier and, dare I say, more loving person.

Forty-eight years ago, life's major questions were answered for me: *Where did I come from? Why am I here? Where am I going?* I realized how much God loved me and how he longed to be engaged in my life. Seventy-two years ago, my earthly father gave me his DNA. In 1971, my heavenly father gave me his Spirit.

As a result, I'm able to stare my past in the face and see that what were disappointments and hardships to me at the time worked out in his good plan for me. (Even the rejection by every sorority on the third day of rush served me well. Mother had told me letters and official recommendations weren't necessary, but they were essential. Had I pledged a sorority and become immersed in a demanding social life, I may have lost touch with Henry Kendall, the second-best thing to ever happen to me.)

Five years ago, I read a book written by a psychologist and a theologian where one portion jumped off the page and nagged me for several days. Dr. Dan B. Allender, one of the coauthors, wrote in *Bold Love:* "I do not believe forgiveness involves forgetting the past and ignoring the damage of past or present harm. To do so, even if it were possible, would be tantamount to erasing one's personal history and the work of God in the midst of our journey."

How does this apply to me? I wondered. The counsel Susan and I received from Dr. Krug regarding our sister had proved to be so wise and practical that I scheduled an appointment with him. I needed assurance or correction that my perspective regarding my history was healthy.

"What brings you in today, Joan?"

"Oh, Bill, I think I'm fine. I have a great husband, our family's dealing with life's blows, and I'm content. But I recently read it's neither desirable nor possible to forget the harm of the past. I'm here to make sure I end well."

So I told him of my harm of the past. I told him about Mother's self-hatred and alcoholism following the abortion when I was a toddler. I told him about the ensuing consequences: her forgetting me at school, the times she embarrassed me, and my desire to murder Ted Hart the night I saw him try to fondle my drunk mother. I told him about Mother and Daddy's vicious arguments and how she disgraced and neglected me.

In the middle of our third consultation, it dawned on me that Daddy, my hero, was culpable too. "I think his enabling and his reactions intensified the sadness in our home."

"Brava, Joan. I was wondering when you'd come to that realization," Dr. Krug said, pleased with my epiphany.

The first real honest-to-goodness telling lasted several more sessions, but I disclosed everything—with empathy and forgiveness for every character involved, including myself—and Dr. Krug declared me healthy.

"Should my daughters know? Would bearing my soul help or harm them?"

"That's a good question," he replied in a pensive manner. "It *was* your life. They're adults with children of their own and capable of appreciating your history. Do you want them to know?"

"Yes, in a way, I do. We all long to be known, don't we? But I'm willing to leave it alone. Besides, they loved their grandmother, though what she contributed were mere morsels from the master's table. But they didn't realize that. How could they know that?"

"I think their knowing could be beneficial, but don't force it," he advised. "Warn them it's not an altogether lovely story. You may have one or two choose not to hear, and that's okay."

On our beach trip the same year, I asked the girls to join me on the porch. Meg and Libby were prepared to hear, but Katie, who adored her grandmother, declined apologetically and went inside. After I divulged our family's past, Meg stood, walked behind me, and wrapped me under her wings, while Libby sat and cried. Several days later, Katie was ready to hear the stories, stories that brought the four of us closer and instilled in them a tenderheartedness and compassion for their grandmother and for me.

Mother said the past never lets us go, and while her statement is a truism, no circumstance—past, present, or future—can destroy me as I place my faith in God to use the hard times to strengthen me and improve the quality of my life and relationships.

I am drawn to Christ because of his love for me. His are the scars of a caring and friendly man who was invited to weddings and turned water into wine. His hands touched people we wouldn't even speak to had we been there. He was welcomed and accepted by outcasts and the most scurrilous of individuals; yet he rebuked the religious leaders who were working their way to heaven without realizing that heaven had come to them. Who couldn't love a man—a God—like that, who comes to us with kindness, truth, and eternal security?

Never capricious, he offered me acceptance when I didn't like myself, and life when I was lifeless. He still woos me at my worst, but I'm not afraid of him. Neither can I hide; he's intimately acquainted with me and all my ways.

The masquerade is over.

If I could write the score of my story, a happy steady tune of a flute plays when Susan appears. A piano, in a minor key, plays with moxie for Linda. Jazz and, on occasion, the doleful tune of an English horn reveals Daddy. Then there's Henry, who requires nothing more than the gentle strumming of a banjo and guitar.

A wistful string section is dominant for Mama with occasional bells, whistles, xylophones, and cymbals to show her wit and charm.

Jadie Bell warrants the entire orchestra.

Night after night, and year after year, I would watch and listen as she knelt beside that pitiful cot at the beach and prayed for me.

Only now, I can say with certainty, "Yes, Jadie Bell, I will see you another day."

Our daughters and their husbands (from left): Dale and Meg Meadows, Katie and Jimmy Pickel, and Libby and Allen House.

Our daughters: (back row from left) me with Katie; front (from left), Libby and Meg.

Our family in 2017.

Our family in 2018.

ACKNOWLEDGMENTS

PROGRESSING FROM THAT PLACE TO THIS PLACE TOOK almost a lifetime, though it need not have. Recounting the long process required four years of writing and reinforcement at every turn.

Throughout the years, friends had laughed and said, "You oughta write a book!" But when someone looked me squarely in the eye and spoke in all seriousness, "You really should write a book," I agreed. However, none of these people knew even the half of it.

People near and far—old friends and strangers—seemed to come out of nowhere to rally around and help me maneuver the octopus-like world of writing. Little did I know the assistance I would need and garner once I determined to pen *Secrets on Saulter Road*.

From the book's conception, Jimbo Head with The Center for Executive Leadership, motivated me to share my story, despite the fact that I spilled coffee all over him at O'Henry's the first time we met and before our conversation ever began.

Loving appreciation to Sara Baugh, a retired system-wide Language Arts and Reading Consultant (Knoxville, TN), who popped on the scene at the perfect time. For two fun years as my first editor, she reminded me, "Show, don't tell!"

Avid readers Brenda and Roger Meadows deserve tribute for reading and commending my clumsy first draft. They found merit in my manuscript when it was but a feeble attempt to put a life into words.

Author Candy Wood Lindley (whom I hadn't seen for many years but then almost tripped over as she sat on the curb by the doctor's office) steered me to the perfect writers' conference and also to Concierge Book Publishing Services. President Lisa Pelto and her team were invaluable and have been skilled and patient partners as I roamed the maze of creating a tangible product. I also wish to express my sincere appreciation to the stealth beta reading team, who deftly pointed out areas in my manuscript that needed a little TLC.

Jane Friedman kindly shared her expert advice regarding details of my course of action.

Andi Cumbo-Floyd's thoughtful and thorough developmental edit proved instrumental in my regrouping, rethinking, and rewriting.

Carol Slaughter, owner of Annabelle's, graciously designed and printed invitations and envelopes for my book launch party.

To my sisters, Linda (now deceased) and Susan, thank you for sharing your memories and for refreshing and correcting mine!

Expressing gratitude to my husband and family will fall short by several thousand words. My biggest champions, Henry and our three daughters and their husbands, have stood by me for four long years, as have my dearest friends who have no doubt often wondered, "Where's Joan?"

My sons-in-law supported me in concrete ways. Jimmy Pickel brought encouragement and a nice bottle of wine each time he and his family visited from Nashville; Dale Meadows, the woodworking enthusiast, created a handsome stand for my first book copy; and Allen House rescued me from numerous technical challenges.

Katie, Meg, and Libby—my cherished daughters—you are my most delightful of companions. Moreover, observing how you love your families and handle life's blows has been the joy of my life and has more than made up for my childhood sadness.

Henry Kendall, you loved me long ago when I thought I was unacceptable, and you never, ever, ever gave up on me. Please know how much I adore and admire you, my steadfast compassionate husband.

Thank you all for investing in me.

ABOUT THE AUTHOR

J OAN KENDALL WAS BORN AND BRED in Birmingham, Alabama. She was a member of the Board of Contributors with *The Birmingham News*. Her work has appeared in *The Citizen Magazine* and the anthology *The Short and Sweet of It*, and she has appeared several times on PBS's *For the Record*.

Joan twice served on the Alabama State Textbook Committee at the request of the governor, and at the request of the state superintendent, she served on

Author photo courtesy of
Heather Durham Photography.

the steering committee of the Alabama Reading Initiative. She has spoken at the Birmingham Civil Rights Institute Conference, Alabama Veterans of Foreign Wars (keynote), Leadership Alabama, Policy Exchange Foundation, and Kiwanis Clubs.

She received a national award for involving the community in education. In 2003, Joan helped launch an after-school program for inner-city children, which is now in over thirty schools serving 2,000 children.

Joan and her husband, Henry, still reside in Birmingham, Alabama, and have three daughters and eight grandchildren.

Made in the USA
Columbia, SC
05 May 2019